The Madame Bovary Blues

Other Books by Stirling Haig

Madame de Lafayette

Sartre and Biography

Flaubert and the Spoken Word: A Study of Dialogue in Four "Modern" Novels

The Madame Bovary Blues

THE PURSUIT OF ILLUSION

IN NINETEENTH-CENTURY

FRENCH FICTION

Stirling Haig

Louisiana State University Press *Baton Rouge and London*

Copyright © 1987 by Louisiana State University Press
All rights reserved
Manufactured in the United States of America

Designer: Patricia Douglas Crowder
Typeface: Linotron 202 Janson
Typesetter: G & S Typesetters, Inc.
Printer: Thomson-Shore, Inc.
Binder: John H. Dekker & Sons

10 9 8 7 6 5 4 3 2 1

LIBRARY OF CONGRESS CATALOGING-IN-PUBLICATION DATA

Haig, Stirling.
The Madame Bovary blues.

Includes bibliographical references and index.
1. French fiction—19th century—History and
criticism.   2. Illusion in literature.   3. Flaubert,
Gustave, 1821–1880. Madame Bovary.   I. Title.
PQ653.H35   1987   843'.7'09   87-3186
ISBN 0-8071-1398-0

Some of the chapters of this book have been published in a somewhat different form in the following publications under the following titles: "The Blue Illusion of *Fromont jeune et Risler aîné*," *Nineteenth-Century French Studies*, VI (Fall–Winter, 1977–78), 111–17; "La Chambre circulaire d'*Indiana*," *Neophilologus*, LXII (October, 1978), 505–12; "Conscience and Anti-Militarism in Vigny's *Servitude et grandeur militaires*," *PMLA*, LXXXIX (January, 1974), 50–56; "La Descente du paradis," *Stendhal Club*, XXI (January 15, 1979), 139–45; "Dualistic Patterns in *La Peau de chagrin*," *Nineteenth-Century French Studies*, I (Summer, 1973), 211–18; "From Cathedral to Book, from Stone to Press: Hugo's Portrait of the Artist in *Notre-Dame de Paris*," *Stanford French Review*, VII (Winter, 1979), 343–50; "Madame Arnoux's *coffret*," *Romanic Review*, LXXV (November, 1984), 469–82; "The *Madame Bovary* Blues," *Romanic Review*, XLI (February, 1970), 27–34; "The Identities of Fabrice del Dongo," *French Studies*, XXVII (April, 1973), 170–76; "The Substance of Illusion in Flaubert's 'Un Coeur simple,'" *Stanford French Review*, VII (Winter, 1983), 301–15; "Sur les orangers de *la Chartreuse de Parme*," *Stendhal Club*, XIV (October 15, 1971), 27–30. The author is grateful to the editors and publishers of these periodicals for permission to use this material.

To my family

La Forme est Peut-être une erreur de tes sens, la Substance une imagination de ta pensée. A moins que le monde étant un flux perpétuel des choses, l'apparence au contraire ne soit tout ce qu'il y a de plus vrai, l'illusion la seule réalité.

Form is an error of your senses perhaps, and Substance imagined by your mind. Unless—the world being a perpetual stream of things— appearance on the contrary is all that is most true, and illusion the sole reality.

—Flaubert, *La Tentation de Saint-Antoine*

Contents

The Madame Bovary Blues

The Absent Chimaera

The Chimaera of mythology was a fire-belching beast with the head and body of a lion, the belly of a goat, and the tail of a dragon. Bellerophon, mounted on Pegasus, slew the Chimaera at the bidding of the king of Lycia. Emboldened by his prowess, Bellerophon attempted to ride Pegasus to the sun. He was punished for his temerity and came to the unhappy end that Homer recounts in the *Iliad*.

Because of its leonine form, the Chimaera is sometimes adduced as the genetrix of the Sphinx and the Nemean lion. Thus the Chimaera is linked to the hero's combat with wild beasts—Bellerophon, Oedipus, Hercules—a standard component of coronation rituals in Greece and Asia Minor. The Christian Saint George, with his lively cult in Greece, is an obvious avatar of the myth.

In French literature Montaigne appears to be the first to mention the *chimère*, while the rational seventeenth century conceived of the word merely as the symmetrical antonym of solid reality. Corneille constantly uses the term in this sense of "vain imagination," and La Fontaine as signifying harmless fancy, insubstantial vagary.

Les chimères, le rien, tout est bon; je soutiens
    Qu'il faut de tout aux entretiens;
C'est un parterre où Flore épand ses biens.

Chimaerae, nothings, all serves; I claim
    That conversation requires a bit of everything:
It is a bed of flowers where Flora sprinkles her riches.

It remains for Rousseau to endow the term with a potential that prepares its nineteenth-century flourishing. In the Ninth Book of the *Confessions* he tells of the second "crisis" of his life, the one that caused the austere Jean-Jacques, at age forty-four, to become anew a *berger extravagant*. In an extraordinary passage that adumbrates the creative fervor he poured into the composition of the *Nouvelle Héloïse*, Rousseau writes:

L'impossibilité d'atteindre aux êtres réels me jetta dans le pays des chiméres, et ne voyant rien d'existant qui fut digne de mon délire, je le nourris dans un monde idéal que mon imagination créatrice eut bientôt peuplé d'êtres selon mon coeur. . . . Oubliant tout à fait la race humaine, je me fis des sociétés de créatures parfaites aussi célestes par leurs vertus que par leurs beautés, d'amis sûrs, tendres, fidelles, tels que je n'en trouve jamais ici bas.

The impossibility of reaching real beings cast me into the land of the chimaera; and seeing nothing in existence that was worthy of my fervor, I nourished it upon an ideal world that my creative imagination had soon peopled with beings of my heart's desire. . . . Completely forgetting the human race, I made for myself societies of perfect creatures, as heavenly in their virtues as their beauty, reliable friends, tender and loyal, such as I never find on this earth.

Here *chimères* is opposed to reality, but with a capital semantic shift. Now illusion is consoling, even redemptive, and marked positively. It is not the product of a vain imagination, but of a *creative* imagination. It is not a "nothing"—rather it compensates for a lack; it fills a sensible, palpable void. The experience of delirium is thus creative—and literary; it demands to be "nourished" on the ideal, on a Kantian ideal.

A few years after this description of what can be called fulsome solitude, in the third of those *Lettres à Malesherbes* of which Sainte-Beuve said he had written nothing more beautiful, Rousseau vaunted the definitive superiority of the imagination, the "golden age of my fantasy," over the insufficiencies of mundane existence: "J'ai cent fois plus joui de mes chimeres qu'ils ne font des réalités" 'I took a hundred times more enjoyment from my chimaerae than they do from reality.'

Rousseau's use of *chimère* would appear to be programmatic as far as the nineteenth century is concerned. In the paradigm of hero versus beast, as reformulated by Rousseau, it requires little effort to discern an emblematic struggle, that of the artist and his quest—his task of capturing and taming the fabulous. The *chimère* is thus a vision demanding to be conquered.

A few of the Romantics would continue to employ *chimère* as a synonym for deception or error. Thus, Eugénie de Guérin writes in a letter of 1839 to warn a friend of the dangers lurking in someone who would cause her to "sauter en croupe avec lui, galopant mille chimères" 'leap on horseback with him, riding to a thousand chimaerae'—an instructive and instrumental usage, since we observe here for the first time the metonymical substitution of the chimaera for Pegasus. Hugo's Don Salluste also warns against fancy: "Leurre! Imagination! Chimère!" (*Ruy Blas*). Hugo would further use the word architecturally, to designate the composite ecclesiastical styles of which Notre-Dame de Paris is a distillation. His poems to Dürer and Dante make use of the word. With the sense of illusion, *chimère* also appears in Senancour's *Rêveries*, Chateaubriand's *Les Martyrs*, and Constant's *Journaux intimes*. (These are all instances of noun usage; adjectivally the word invariably has a deprecatory sense.)

Yet, in a faint echo of Rousseau, Balzac wrote in the famous Avant-propos to the *Comédie humaine* that the initial inspiration for his panoramic enterprise was at first a "chimère." Balzac was obviously not referring to a passing caprice but to a stupefying—and (for him) ineluctable—undertaking of great magnitude. The divine capacity for self-deception, the thirst for the ideal that Rousseau had exalted as a compensation for the disappointments of life, would course unslaked through nineteenth-century French literature, from Romanticism through Realism and Symbolism, in both prose and poetry. Even in the period of high Naturalism, Zola would renounce the world and penetrate into an (earthly) garden of delights in *La Faute de l'abbé Mouret*—the only novel by Zola that continued to command the admiration of those like Barbey d'Aurevilly and Huysmans who had rejected the master's lesson. But let us return to literary chronology.

In *La Chartreuse de Parme*, Stendhal pairs two very different sorts of heroines and sets them as rivals for his hero's love. They are the sprightly, worldly Duchesse de Sanseverina and the aloof, ethereal Clélia Conti. Their respective profane and religious temperaments are initially figured in painterly comparisons: Clélia's lyrical spirituality is out of Guido Reni's classical shapes, while the duchess has the voluptuous smile and tender melancholy of Leonardo's Herodias figures: "Autant la duchesse était sémillante, pétillante d'esprit et de malice . . . autant Clélia se montrait calme et lente à s'émouvoir, soit par mépris de ce qui l'entourait soit par regret de quelque chimère absente" 'Just as the duchess was sprightly, sparkling with wit and mischievousness . . . Clélia was calm and slow to show emotion, either out of disdain for her surroundings or regret for some absent chimaera.'

Les Chimères, as the title of Nerval's masterpiece, summarizes the mystic and amorous ideal proceeding from his religious syncretism. It is the symbol of his *supernaturalisme*, his ideal of transcendence, to use the term he himself employed in the preface to *Les Filles du feu*. At approximately the same time, Baudelaire was using the term *surnaturalisme* and describing in a poem of the Orphic tradition ("Bohémiens en voyage") the dreary march of the human caravan across the sands of time.

> Promenant sur le ciel des yeux appesantis
> Par le morne regret des chimères absentes.
>
> Scanning the sky with eyes heavy
> With dejected regret for the absent chimaerae.

In *Réalisme et idéalisme* (a revealing title) Delacroix laments "La matière retombe toujours dans la tristesse" 'The material always slips back into sadness,' and in *La Bohème* Rodolfo's famous "soave fanciulla" aria explains for Mimi his carefree existence as a poet.

> Per sogni e per chimere
> e per castelli in aria
> l'anima ho milionaria.
>
> In dreams and chimaerae
> And in castles in the air,
> My soul is a millionaire.

The Chimaera, it will be observed, has usurped the place of Pegasus in modern reformulations of the myth, losing in its passage all vestige of monsterdom, of horror, while retaining only the signifieds of the fabulous—and thus the fictitious and the artistic. And Bellerophon, through his failed attempt to fly to the sun, has become one with the modernized figure of the artist: Icarus. The entire myth has been assimilated to a creative, consoling flight of the imagination, the latter no longer a source of error, as it had been for Antiquity and in the French Classics, but of intuitive truth. And the homeland of the new Chimaera, as I attempt to show in the title essay of this book, is the "blue" dreamworld.

I 🖾 Distortions of Desire in Balzac's

La Peau de chagrin

La Peau de chagrin, more than the traditionally cited *Les Chouans*, is the novel that foreshadows most profoundly the works of Balzac's maturity. This can be seen in its use of the flashback and in the characters' passionate fixations—their absorption with historical instability and social erosion. But the assertion can also be demonstrated by sheer chronology, for most of Balzac's key novels follow *La Peau de chagrin* within a six-year span. Between 1831 and 1837, Balzac published (among others) the following titles, which are by turn dramatically or philosophically oriented: *Le Chef-d'oeuvre inconnu, Louis Lambert, Eugénie Grandet, Le Père Goriot, Séraphîta, Le Lys dans la vallée*, and the beginning of *Illusions Perdues*. Any teacher will recognize in these titles the basic texts for a course on Balzac.

If today we increasingly recognize in *La Peau de chagrin* the very core of the Balzacian universe, this is not to say that it has ever been a neglected novel (if indeed it is possible for one of Balzac's novels to be neglected).[1] Félix Davin, who for a period

1. See F. W. J. Hemmings' incisive monograph, *Balzac: An Interpretation of La Comédie Humaine* (New York, 1967); Linda Rudich, "Une Interprétation de 'La Peau de chagrin,'" *L'Année Balzacienne* (1971), 205–33; François Bilodeau, *Balzac et le jeu des mots* (Montréal, 1971).

was Balzac's literary collaborator, or rather, literary *âme damnée*, summed up the subject of the novel as neatly as anyone should hope to, in the 1836 preface to the *Etudes Philosophiques:* "Life diminishes in direct ratio to the intensity of desire or the dissipation of thought." This single sentence is the direct forerunner of virtually all criticism on *La Peau de chagrin*, including François Bilodeau's discussion of "the law of contrasts" and "the linking of opposites" in his *Balzac et le jeu des mots.* And every reader of *La Peau de chagrin* has been sensible of the fundamental thematic oppositions of the book: illusion and reality, possession and contemplation, knowledge and action, desire and death, power and duration, all of which are bound in an antinomic or dualistic symbol, the magic skin. Obvious also are certain paired opposites: Foedora, the incarnation of heartless society, is paired (through Raphaël) with Pauline, the loving individual; the antiquary's philosophy is the reverse of that of Aquilina and Euphrasie; less obvious, but certainly no less visible, are other contradictory modes that can only be related by means of Balzac's questing, dualistic vision.

To take one small shred of novelistic detail, we can note that the skin itself is both stiff and pliable, and at one point it is described as being "semblable à une feuille de métal par son peu de flexibilité" 'similar to a sheet of metal in its inflexibility.'[2] Yet, a few pages later it has acquired an "incroyable ductilité" 'incredible pliableness.' Near the end of the novel, during the episode in which the skin is subjected to various scientific analyses and remedies, Raphaël is terrified by "la souplesse de la peau quand il la maniait, mais sa dureté lorsque les moyens de destruction mis à la disposition de l'homme étaient dirigés sur elle. . . . Ce fait incontestable lui donnait le vertige" (247) 'the skin's suppleness when he handled it, but its hardness when the means of destruction available to man were brought to bear on it. . . . This indisputable fact made him feel dizzy.'[3] Inasmuch

2. Honoré de Balzac, *La Peau de chagrin*, ed. Maurice Allem (Classiques Garnier ed.; Paris, 1955), 36. All page references in the text are to this edition.
3. This "fact," incidentally, leads some of the scientists to proclaim their belief in God, others in the devil (246).

as this episode is intended to demonstrate the insufficiencies of science when confronted with the deeper mysteries of life, we may also conclude that the skin is a symbol of ineluctable human destiny. Like Oedipus or Raphaël de Valentin, men can entertain the illusion that they are "handling" or manipulating their fates, but they cannot basically alter or destroy them.[4] And all lives have destinies for Balzac, destinies that are inherently dramatic: they are spectacle and parade, and they form the human comedy, of which Balzac is as much audience as he is director.

By temperament and vision, Balzac is very different from later French novelists. Balzac could write intimate biofictions like *César Birotteau* and *Le Curé de campagne;* he could not have conceived of the detached pathological inquest of *Une Vie.* Consider the disparity and paradox, long after Balzac's death, of Michel Lévy's simultaneous publication in 1869 of definitive versions of both *Splendeurs et Misères des courtisanes* and *L'Education sentimentale:* the dramatic "last incarnation" of Vautrin and the suicides of Lucien de Rupembré and Esther Gobseck contrast starkly with the pseudoevents and the repetitive aimlessness that shrivel the existence of Frédéric Moreau. Whereas Balzac's characters expend and consume their energies in orgiastic tableaux, Flaubert's husband theirs and transform them into nostalgic dream-memories. Flaubert's characters and their present are freighted with the self-reinforcing accretions of a recycled past, but the past of Balzac's characters, debouching into their present like a massive confluent, roils their existence. Nostalgia, inconclusiveness, and potential dominate in the one, expense and fulfillment in the other. Yet, as both titles imply, each involves a shedding of illusions, a ritual passage and coming to terms with loss.

All this is not to say that Balzac's omniscient technique im-

---

4. It is interesting to note Balzac's pessimistic formulation of man's "end," *i.e.*, death, in *La Peau de chagrin.* Death is consistently viewed in terms of suicide. As the skin abolishes time and duration, there are either *slow* suicides (the *antiquaire* and his claimed age of 102 years) or *rapid* suicides (the quick death of Raphaël). In the language of the gambling den, this is the "name of the game": one's odds are either long or short.

plies a qualitatively deeper (or more superficial) vision than does Flaubert's ostensibly limited point of view, but to point out how much Balzac deals in contrasts, to underscore once more the Proustian dictum that "le style, pour l'écrivain aussi bien que pour le peintre, est une question non de technique, mais de vision." 'style for the writer, just as much as for the painter, is a question not of technique, but of vision.'[5] Yet it is principally the technical expression of Balzac's contrastive vision that I propose to examine, rather than dwell upon its dualistic nature.

The beginning of *La Peau de chagrin* abounds in random ironies and contrasts, all apparently as different as chalk from cheese. Balzac takes great pains to describe the antithesis between the displays of gold in the gaming room and the physical deterioration of the surroundings. The sudden, abrupt gestures of the impassive bettors, as they mark the passes of red or black, are punctuated with cries of "oui" and "non," and Balzac—as ?' ways—provides a fetching *explicatus*.

Cette antithèse humaine se découvre partout où l'âme réagit puissamment sur elle-même. L'amoureux veut mettre sa maîtresse dans la soie, la revêtir d'un moelleux tissu d'Orient, et, la plupart du temps, il la possède sur un grabat. L'ambitieux se rêve au faîte du pouvoir, tout en s'aplatissant dans la boue du servilisme. Le marchand végète au fond d'une boutique humide et malsaine, en élevant un vaste hôtel, d'où son fils, héritier précoce, sera chassé par une licitation fraternelle. Enfin, existe-t-il chose plus déplaisante qu'une maison de plaisir? Singulier problème! Toujours en opposition avec lui-même, trompant ses espérances par ses maux présents, et ses maux par un avenir qui ne lui appartient pas, l'homme imprime à tous ses actes le caractère de l'inconséquence et de la faiblesse. (6)

This human antithesis is to be found in every situation where the soul reacts powerfully upon itself. The lover wants to put his mistress in silk, to cover her in soft Oriental fabrics, and most of the time, he possesses her on a straw pallet. The ambitious man vegetates in the back of a damp, foul shop, while raising a huge townhouse from which his son, a precocious heir, will be expelled by a brotherly lawsuit. Finally, is there anything more unpleasant than a house of pleasure? Singular problem! Always opposed to himself, betraying his hopes by his current wrongdoing, and his wrongdoing by a future he doesn't own, man imprints inconsistency and weakness upon all his acts.

5. Marcel Proust, *A la recherche du temps perdu* (Pléiade ed.; 3 vols.; Paris, 1959), 895.

The outcome of the gambling scene is well known: Raphaël loses his last napoleon—the symbolic coin of the generation of 1830—and is about to commit suicide by throwing himself into the Seine. Here he is seized by a series of contradictory actions and observations. He finds himself carefully brushing off his clothes. Penniless, he is asked for alms—*la carità*—by two beggars, one young, one old. Upon seeing the buildings of the "Secours aux asphyxiés" (the emergency service), he reflects that alive he is a social zero, dead a corpse worth fifty francs. Destitute, on foot, shabbily dressed, he attempts to throw a last "piercing glance" in the direction of an obviously rich young lady, elegantly turned out in satin and rolling in a "brilliant équipage" (15). In a somewhat hallucinatory mood he gazes at various Parisian monuments that seem subject to "d'inexplicables caprices de laideur et de beauté" (16) 'inexplicable caprices of ugliness and beauty.' This mood continues as he wanders into the antique shop, his blood "tantôt bouillonnant comme une cascade, tantôt tranquille et fade comme l'eau tiède" (17) 'now boiling like a waterfall, now still and flat as lukewarm water.' Raphaël, as Balzac notes, is either drunk on life or drunk on death: "N'était-il pas ivre de la vie, ou peut-être de la mort!" (16) 'Was he not drunk on life, or perhaps on death!'

There is always hyperbole, enumeration, stylistic proliferation in Balzac, but we can discern in this series of contrasts larger, "philosophical" groupings that can be called worlds of life and worlds of death, with Raphaël standing squarely between them. On one hand is the world of luxury and enjoyment of the young woman; on the other, the world of decay and abstention of the antiquary. In parallel fashion, in the very first pages of the novel, we have the world of the gaming table (which stands for gain, fulfillment, and potential) and that of suicide (which stands for obliteration and nothingness).

As Peter Brooks has pointed out, *La Peau de chagrin* stands as an anticipatory fable of the troubling dialectic of desire and death that Freud was to analyze nearly a hundred years later in his study of post–World War I trauma: "Nearly the whole of Freud's argument in *Beyond the Pleasure Principle* is allegorized

here: in Raphaël's discovery that with the possession of total realization of desire, the self encounters the impossibility of desir-
ing, because to desire becomes, and can only be, the choice of
death of that same self. The talisman contracts in itself and
phantasmatically represents the paradoxical logic of Freud's essay: that Eros is subtended by the death instinct, the drive of
living matter to return to the quiescence of the inorganic, a state
prior to life."[6]

With Raphaël's entrance into the antique shop, there is a
marked intensification of antitheses and contrasts, but whereas
prior to this point their arrangement has been a semirandom,
horizontal presentation, the arrangement is now a vertical, pyra-
midal structure that is clearly one of a ritual initiation, mystical
in nature. Raphaël's journey from the ground floor to the *troisième étage* is an ascension and transcendence of the chaos and
debris of civilizations past and present, an "Apocalypse rétro-
grade" (25) leading to a revelation or synthesis.[7] That the scene
is leading up to such a unifying discovery may also be deduced
from mention of two key figures central to Balzac's imaginative
and creative patterns, Cuvier and Bernard Palissy. There are
numerous allusions to Bernard Palissy in Balzac's novels. For
Balzac, the creative experimenter who fired his own furniture
in support of his inventions and researches in ceramics (the very
first object seen in the shop is "un poêle dont les merveilles
étaient dues au génie de Bernard Palissy" 'a stove whose mar-
vels were due to the genius of Bernard Palissy') is the historical
antecedent and symbol of the *recherche de l'absolu* (the search for
the absolute), of the Balthazar Claës, the Frenhofers, the Louis
Lamberts of the *Comédie humaine*, who are all in search of some
unitary principle in creation, just as were, in Balzac's own time,
the naturalists and paleontologists Cuvier and Geoffroy Saint-
Hilaire, the scientific counterparts of these characters.

The details of this "fumier philosophique" 'philosophical

6. Peter Brooks, *Reading for the Plot: Design and Intention in Narrative* (New York,
1984), 50–51.
7. See the mention of "Saint Jean dans Pathmos" (19).

dungheap,' the baubles and knickknacks of the antique shop, remain tightly and dualistically structured; they are opposing elements held together in a synthetic relationship. Consider the apparent jumble of this description:

> Un tournebroche était posé sur un ostensoir, un sabre républicain sur une haquebute du moyen âge. Mme du Barry, peinte au pastel par Latour, une étoile sur la tête, nue et dans un nuage, paraissait contempler avec concupiscence une chibouque indienne, en cherchant à deviner l'utilité des spirales qui serpentaient vers elle.
> Les instruments de mort, poignards, pistolets curieux, armes à secret, étaient jetés pêle-mêle avec des instruments de vie: soupières en porcelaine, assiettes de Saxe, tasses diaphanes venues de Chine, salières antiques, drageoirs féodaux. (18)

> A roasting spit was lying on a monstrance, a republican saber on a medieval harquebus. In a Latour pastel Mme du Barry, a star on her head and nude in a cloud, appeared to be lustfully contemplating an Indian waterpipe, seeking to divine the purpose of the spirals circling toward her.
> Death-dealing instruments—daggers, odd pistols, secret weapons—were heaped pell-mell with life-giving instruments: porcelain soup tureens, Dresden china, China cups, ancient saltcellars, feudal drageoirs.

The instruments of life and death are directly explained and invite an interpretation by contrast with the remaining objects. In the *tournebroche* and the *ostensoir* we can see the sacred and the profane, or the sublime and the ridiculous; in the *sabre républicain* and the *haquebute*, the republic and the monarchy, or the ancient and the modern; in Mme du Barry and the *chibouque indienne*, the Occident and the Orient, or the reveries of the flesh and those of the mind—the dream and death. The permutations are endless, and they are meant to be sociologically inclusive as well, for they take in the traditional estates of society—they include the soldier's tobacco pouch, the priest's ciborium, and the plumes of a throne (18). They are also meant to blaze the path of Western history: as Raphaël moves from room to room and floor to floor, he passes by statues and paintings that belong, in the order cited, to the historical periods of ancient Egypt, Moses and the Hebrews, classical Greece, imperial Rome, Christian Rome, the Middle Ages, the Renaissance, and so on. At the summit of his mystical itinerary through time and space, capsulizing human history with its achievements, follies, and failures, Raphaël perches exhaustedly on a "chaise curule" (26), the *sella curulis* of antiquity, the ivory seat symbolizing the power and investiture of Roman magistrates and notables. Here revelation awaits him with the emergence of the antique dealer, who comes like a red sphere from the depths of the surrounding darkness, the "ténèbres." The antique dealer, or *vieillard*, is himself a study in contrasts, particularly of life and death.

La robe ensevelissait le corps comme dans un vaste linceul, et ne permettait de voir d'autre forme humaine qu'un visage étroit et pâle. Sans le bras décharné, qui ressemblait à un bâton sur lequel on aurait posé une étoffe . . . ce visage aurait paru suspendu dans les airs. . . . Un peintre aurait, avec deux expressions différentes et en deux coups de pinceau, fait de cette figure une belle image du Père éternel ou le masque ricaneur du Méphistophélès.

The robe entombed his body as if in an enormous shroud, and of the human form allowed only a glimpse of a narrow, ashen face. Without the bony arm, which looked like a cloth-covered stick . . . the face would have appeared to be suspended in space. . . . A painter, with two different expressions and in two brushstrokes, would have drawn from that visage a fine figure of the eternal Father or the sneering mask of Mephistopheles.

The *vieillard*, with his Moses-like "Judaic head," discourses on wisdom and knowledge and tempts Raphaël with the fatal skin, which combines "VOULOIR ET POUVOIR" 'WILL AND POWER.' Raphaël, of course, with his past of failure and destitution and with the composition of a *Théorie de la volonté* behind him, is quick to accept the Faustian pact that rushes him to his death.

Students often ask why Raphaël, once in possession of the skin, does not simply wish for eternal life. An answer they will accept is that the skin can have no salvatory, redemptive power. For the skin is a symbol of *earthly* destiny and has no metaphysical overtones. This assertion can be justified by the very dualistic scheme that we have seen, for within this pattern the place of the skin itself is a highly significant one. The skin hangs on a wall directly opposite a portrait of Christ by Raphael (Raffaello)—a wall "facing the portrait." The skin then is paired, within the series of matching opposites, with Christ the Redeemer. If Christ is the resurrection and life, then the skin—its paired opposite—cannot bring eternal life. Christ is life (or the Life), but as the *vieillard* warns Raphaël, the skin is only another form of suicide.

Raphaël's first words upon seizing the skin are, "Eh bien, oui, je veux vivre avec excès!" 'Yes, then, I shall live with excess!' As Balzac later explains at some length, "Tous les excès sont frères" (178) 'All excesses are related.' There are excesses of abstention just as there are excesses of indulgence. Thus the *vieillard*, despite his theory of *savoir*, can no more escape his end than can Raphaël. Raphaël vengefully and somewhat petulantly wishes a life of debauchery on the *vieillard* and will not see him again until much later, at the end of the novel, and then it is in the company of Euphrasie, the courtesan-danseuse (211). The fulfillment of this particular wish is not to be read as proving once again the puissance of the skin, but as the inevitability of fate, regardless of the stratagems adopted to exorcize it. Balzac has deliberately delayed the reader's knowledge of the realization of this wish the better to set it next to Raphaël's equally garish end. Balzac, like Ecclesiastes, is asking, "And how dieth the wise man?" And the answer is, "As the fool."

In fact, we should note that from the moment that the skin makes its appearance, Raphaël and the *vieillard* move toward a similar end while following opposite paths: Raphaël moves from debauchery to deprivation, the *vieillard* from deprivation to debauchery. "Tous les excès sont frères."

The *peau de chagrin* is power; through the immediate, even anticipated gratification of desire, it is power that abolishes time, and thus duration or longevity, and that leads straight to wear, to attrition, to shrinkage, to the erosion of life by life. The *peau de chagrin*, viewed as a magic purveyor of satisfactions, is really a false synthesis of the age-old interplay of desire and death. There is no synthesis to Balzac's dualistic vision—there is only the relationship of excess. Or to conclude with an elliptical linguistic paradigm and pun of fate, which is borrowed from Rabelais and forms one of *La Peau de chagrin*'s leitmotifs—"*Carymary, Carymara.*"

II ‹ From Cathedral to Book, from Stone

to Press: Hugo's Portrait of the Artist in

Notre-Dame de Paris

Recent interpretations of Hugo's novel have suggested that the work's interest and unity are to be found in the concept of myth or romance and that the action of *Notre-Dame* turns about a central character, identified now as Claude Frollo, now as Quasimodo.[1] Although such readings unquestionably lay open new dimensions and critical perspectives, they cannot entirely replace more traditional, or perhaps "orthodox" views, which put the cathedral itself squarely in the center of the work's historical and dramatic interest.[2] Indeed, the cathedral's very mass, the sheer temporal and geographical space that it occupies in the novel, would be difficult to ignore or displace. The text speaks

---

*This chapter is a revision of an article that appeared in the Winter, 1979, issue of *Stanford French Review*, published by Anma Libri.

1. Richard B. Grant, *The Perilous Quest: Image, Myth, and Prophecy in the Narratives of Victor Hugo* (Durham, N.C., 1968); Kathryn E. Wildgen, "Romance and Myth in *Notre-Dame de Paris*," *French Review*, XLIX (1976), 319–27.

2. Raouf Simaika, *L'Inspiration épique dans les romans de Victor Hugo* (Geneva, 1962), 44. Already Sainte-Beuve had stated that "art, architecture, and the cathedral" were the inspirations of the work. He also shrewdly observed that a sinister light seemed to rise from below, to project an "infernal" illumination on the cathedral. Sainte-Beuve, *Critiques et portraits littéraires* (5 vols.; Paris, 1836), II, 143. For F. B. Kirsch, the cathedral is a magnet; see Kirsch, "Die Struktur von *Notre-Dame de Paris* in Lichte des Kathedralensymbol," *Zeitschrift für Französische Sprache und Literatur*, LXXVIII (1968), 10–34.

for it—in the title, in the introduction, in the whole Livre Troisième, in the denouement, in the elusive theme of *ananke*. And
throughout, the cathedral is figured in the ubiquitous sign of
Notre-Dame de Paris, the stone.

The stone is the petrification of the medieval world and its
characteristic theocracy; the stone is its fate, its death. To the
ethereal heights of the church, Victor Hugo could have apposed
the magic lightness of La Esmeralda's dance, which suggests
heights and the flight of the magic carpet: "Elle dansait, elle
tournait, elle tourbillonnait sur un vieux tapis de Perse, jeté
négligemment sous ses pieds"[3] 'She danced, she turned, she
whirled on an old Persian carpet casually thrown beneath her
feet.' For La Esmeralda's domain *is* height, and escape from
gravity. The curious literally seize ladders the better to observe
her dancing, and after her *mariage au pot cassé* with Gringoire,
Hugo will designate her as an "être aérien" 'an airy being' (114).
For weeks she will find asylum in the perches of Notre-Dame
itself. But Hugo's purpose is, in the end, to prepare for a particularly dramatic and brutal reversal of these ascensional motifs, and this peripety is associated with the stone from which
both church and gibbet are made. For La Esmeralda, "l'asile
était une prison comme une autre" (417) 'the asylum was just
like any prison,' and she will last be seen dancing at the end of a
rope, hanging from one of the numerous stone gibbets of fif-
teenth-century Paris and bearing all the grisly weight of the
executioner pressing down upon her delicate neck.

Quasimodo qui ne respirait plus depuis quelques instants vit se balancer
au bout de la corde, à deux toises au-dessus du pavé, la malheureuse enfant *avec l'homme accroupi les pieds sur ses épaules.* La corde fit plusieurs tours
sur elle-même, et Quasimodo vit courir d'horribles convulsions le long du
corps de l'égyptienne. (562, italics added)

Quasimodo, who had been holding his breath for several moments, saw
the unfortunate girl swinging from the end of the rope, two or three yards

---

3. Victor Hugo, *Notre-Dame de Paris*, ed. M.-F. Guyard (Paris, 1966), 74. All page
references in the text are to this edition. This description of La Esmeralda contains two
further touches in which the affective link, or seme, is flight: the "wasp" and her "robe
bariolée qui *se gonflait*" (75) 'many colored gown that was swelling in the wind.'

above the pavement, *the man squatting with his feet on her shoulders.* The rope spun around several turns, and Quasimodo saw horrible convulsions running up and down the length of the gypsy's body. (italics added)

This scene is focalized through the anguished observation of Claude Frollo and Quasimodo standing on the towers of Notre-Dame and looking down, across the Seine, to the place de Grève—from afar and above.

Descent, fall, and stone are replicated in Frollo's death. Pushed by Quasimodo, his weight will bend the lead gutter (the tombal metal) and plunge him into the realm of stone-death: "Tout était pierre autour de lui: devant ses yeux, les monstres béants; au-dessous, tout au fond, dans la place, le pavé; au-dessus de sa tête, Quasimodo qui pleurait" (564) 'All was stone around him: before his eyes, the gaping monsters; below, right at the bottom in the square, the pavement above his head, the weeping Quasimodo.' Frollo does not fall straight down, but hits first the slate roof of a nearby house, where he becomes as a stone ("tuile" 'slate') that falls on stone: "Il glissa rapidement sur le toit comme une tuile qui se détache, et alla rebondir sur le pavé. Là, il ne remua plus" (565) 'He slipped rapidly on the roof like a slate coming loose, and bounced onto the pavement. There he moved no more.' In the course of his fall Claude Frollo is not so much crushed as he is petrified.[4]

Quasimodo's tears, in this chapter, the last in which the characters are seen alive, humanize him in extremis, but he, too, undergoes an analogous death: having descended into the cave of a vast stone ossuary to embrace the dead Esmeralda, he turns into a calcified skeleton that "falls into dust" (569) at first touch.

Thus, the cathedral—centralizing locus of the novel's action—and its stones determine the register of the characters' *ananke*. The word itself is engraved on the walls of Notre-Dame. If it has disappeared from the walls through scraping or cleaning, it has nevertheless been preserved by the very element that

---

4. His fall accomplishes his earlier prediction of stone-death (75). In addition, one of the *truands* besieging Notre Dame had earlier mistaken Quasimodo for Sabnac, the demon of fortifications, who "changes men into stone and builds towers with them" (478).

succeeds stone and "kills" it, the book—the book, that is, being written by Victor Hugo: "Ainsi, hormis le fragile souvenir que lui consacre l'auteur de ce livre, il ne reste plus rien aujourd'hui du mot mystérieux gravé dans la sombre tour de Notre-Dame" (3) 'Thus, save the fragile memory that the author of this book devotes to it, nothing remains today of the mysterious word carved into the dark tower of Notre-Dame.' The writer of the hand-graven word—*manuscript*—has been "effaced," as has the word *ananke* itself, as may be effaced one day the church itself. But the book subsists: "C'est sur ce mot qu'on a fait ce livre" (4) 'Upon that word this book is based.'

That this world is dead and removed from living concerns is perhaps the basis of Hugo's constant interventions into his narrative, ruptures that continually remind us that the world of Quasimodo, La Esmeralda, and Claude Frollo is firmly in the past. Hugo's technique on this point is precisely the opposite of that of the traditional historical novelist, who strives to make us forget the temporal abyss. Hugo's interventions underscore that chasm, as they refer us exclusively to present or recent history. The comparisons emphasize, in other words, the presence of the gap, rather than its absence: "Si Gringoire vivait de nos jours, quel beau milieu il tiendrait entre le classique et le romantique!" (86) 'If Gringoire were alive today, what a fine middle ground he would occupy between the classic and the Romantic!'; "Si nous n'étions pas au quinzième siècle, nous dirions que Gringoire était descendu de Michel-Ange à Callot" (99) 'If we weren't in the fifteenth century, we would say that Gringoire had descended from Michelangelo to Callot'; "ce qui procura à Gringoire . . . une sensation à peu près pareille à celle qu'é-prouverait Micromégas" (123) 'which brought Gringoire . . . a sensation about like the one that Micromégas might feel'; "Qu'on arrange ces choses comme on pourra. Je ne suis qu'historien" (281) 'Let these matters be settled as best they can. I'm only a historian'; "J'ADORE CORALIE. 1823. SIGNÉ UGÈNE. *Signé* est dans le texte" (graffito, 305) 'I ADORE CORALIE. 1823. SIGNED UGENE. *Signed* is in the text'; "un escalier aussi roide qu'un alexandrin classique" (455) 'a staircase straight as a Classical alexandrine.'[5]

Hugo's *idée-force*, which he wished to place in the very center of *Notre-Dame de Paris*, is in the cathedral and in the second chapter of Livre Cinquième, entitled "CECI TUERA CELA" 'THIS WILL KILL THAT.' First spoken by Claude Frollo in the preceding chapter (207), this banal phrase, composed of prosaic and hardly fatidic demonstratives, is tersely parsed in the following manner: "Ceci tuera cela. Le livre tuera l'édifice" (209) 'This will kill that. The book will kill the edifice.' The thought is two-sided, according to Hugo.

The regret and chagrin that accompany Frollo's fateful utterance are the stunned fear of the priest, whose sacerdotal functions and investiture are menaced by the book. The printed word is likened to the angel Legion, and anticipating Mallarmé's "siècle épouvanté de n'avoir pas connu / Que la mort triomphait dans cette voix!" it is the voice of doom whose six million wings will muffle the voice of the pulpit and the nonprinted word: "C'était la voix du prophète qui entend déjà bruire et fourmiller l'humanité émancipée, qui voit dans l'avenir l'intelligence saper la foi, l'opinion détrôner la croyance, le monde secouer Rome" (209) 'It was the cry of the prophet who could already hear the noise and stir of emancipated humanity, who sees in the future intellect sapping faith, public opinion dethroning belief, the world shaking off Rome.'

The corollary of the thought concerns not the priest but rather—still according to Hugo—the savant and the artist. To the change of form in expression corresponds something deeper, which he likens to new articulations of humanity. Hugo first explains this in a somewhat simplistic way: "le livre de pierre . . . allait faire place au livre de papier. . . . L'imprimerie tuera l'architecture" (210) 'the book of stone . . . was about to give way to the book of paper. . . . Printing will kill architecture.' In the beginning was the Word. Yet, for a secularizing Hugo, it was

---

5. Several of these markers of authorial presence bring Gringoire into Hugo's France of the nineteenth century, a phenomenon that owes nothing to chance, as will soon be shown.

made not flesh but stony, granitic syllables: "Le dolmen et le cromlech celtes, le tumulus étrusque, le galgal hébreu sont des mots" (211) 'The Celtic dolmen and cromlech, the Etruscan tumulus, the Hebrew galgal are words'; Karnak is a whole sentence. And the stones change—they are not capable solely of raising the Temple and the Law. If Romanesque architecture is a theocratic masonry exuding "l'autorité, l'unité, l'impénétrable, l'absolu, Grégoire VII" 'authority, unity, the impenetrable, the absolute, Gregory VII,' the Gothic brings the odor of the masses, and issues in the era of Jacqueries and popular revolts. The Gothic brings a new discourse. It embodies still the sacerdotal mysteries, but it also writes or carves its own subversion—liberty, democracy. "Toute civilisation commence par la théologie et finit par la démocratie" (212) 'Every civilization begins in theology and ends in democracy.' The new text blows revolutionary; Hugo's thoughts here anticipate Bakhtin's concept of *dialogism:* beside the code of the established order, the polyphonic revolutionary text makes a second discourse heard, and this one contests the order it expresses. And so, for Hugo, the poet of the Gothic era makes himself an architect—the dogmatic edifice has fallen into his domain. So long as the priest has his basilica and his altar, "l'artiste la bâtit à sa guise. Adieu le mystère, le mythe, la loi. Voici la fantaisie et le caprice" (214) 'the artist builds it as he pleases. Farewell mystery, myth, and law. Welcome fantasy and caprice.' And here, too, is where the much-maligned character of Pierre Gringoire comes in. Yet, his day has not entirely come. An older order must first die. We are in the fifteenth century, and the printed word's epoch will not arrive until the sixteenth: Luther and the Reformation are inconceivable without their precursor, Gutenberg (210).

CECI TUERA CELA sends us back to reread the great descriptive and historical chapter on Notre-Dame itself (Livre Troisième, Chapter 1). There Hugo emphasized, to an insistent degree, the *mixed* character of the edifice. The cathedral was neither entirely Romanesque nor entirely Gothic. It was a hybrid, an unfinished work—*pendent opera interrupta*—an "édifice de la transition" (131). No longer a Romanesque church and not yet a Gothic one, Notre-Dame could not be classified. Among the old churches of Paris, Notre-Dame is "une sorte de chimère; elle a la tête de l'une, les membres de celle-là, la croupe de l'autre; quelque chose de toutes" (132) 'a sort of chimaera; it possesses the head of this one, the limbs of that one, the croup of the other; something of all of them.'

Hugo thus stresses that the dying world of Claude Frollo—of the stone-writ book, that is, the cathedral itself—is the principal manifestation of the struggle against *ananke* in the novel. (In the preface to *Les Travailleurs de la mer*, Hugo cites triple *anankes*, and *Notre-Dame de Paris* as representing the "ananke of dogmas.") Notre-Dame *shows* liberty succeeding dogmatism; it is a visualization of fatality and obstacle. That Hugo should view both cathedral and book as successive embodiments of man's tongues, voices, and messages is underscored by the repetition of the Babelic analogy. In the chapter "Notre-Dame," architecture is figured as the beehive (132). The link with CECI TUERA CELA is emphasized by the return of the same image, this time with the printed word as the second term of the analogy. After a long architectural-literary passage evoking Shakespeare's "cathedral" and Byron's "mosque," in which the notion of the literary edifice is paramount, Hugo ends his chapter with a comparison of printed works to a new Tower of Babel.

> Certes, c'est là aussi une construction qui grandit et s'amoncelle en spirales sans fin; là aussi il y a confusion de langues, activité incessante, labeur infatigable, concours acharné de l'humanité tout entière, refuge promis à l'intelligence contre un nouveau déluge, contre une submersion de barbares. C'est la seconde tour de Babel du genre humain. (224)

To be sure, this too is a construction that gathers and grows in endless spirals; here too there is a confusion of tongues, incessant activity, untiring labor, the eager collaboration of all humanity, a refuge promised to intellect against a new flood, against a deluge of barbarians. It is the second Tower of Babel of the human race.[6]

6. The whole passage, evoking the labyrinthine structures of the imagination, recalls "Puits de l'Inde!" The image of the cathedral-work of art, needless to say, looks forward to Proust and Combray's Saint-Hilaire.

Claude Frollo and Quasimodo, and Esmeralda too, are lives whose destinies are linked to Notre-Dame's, the stone cathedral of death. Its destiny weighs upon them and crushes them. Their deaths do not signal the end of witchcraft, alchemy, or monsterdom. But at least two of them are the tutelary gods of the cathedral whose "book" is dying. The legacy of this old, moribund world, this book, falls into the possession of an unworthy heir— Pierre Gringoire.

Who else do we perceive in transports of rapturous contemplation before the aesthetic beauties of architectural monuments than Gringoire, whose artistic endeavors suggest the uncertain, unpredictable infancy of the printed word? Gringoire is an *incunabulum;* he frets in the cradle of art. In the scene just alluded to (Livre Dixième, Chapter 1), Gringoire is busy applying himself to composing a commentary on a work not insignificantly entitled *De cupa petrarum,* and is seen "reading" a richly sculpted chapel near Saint-Germain-l'Auxerrois: "il y a un lien intime entre l'hermétique et la maçonnerie. Gringoire avait passé de l'amour d'une idée à l'amour de la forme de cette idée" (442) 'there is a close link between the hermetic and stonework. Gringoire had moved from the love of an idea to the love of the form of that idea.' And when asked by Claude Frollo if he is happy, he responds: "En honneur, oui! J'ai d'abord aimé des femmes, puis des bêtes. Maintenant j'aime des pierres" (443) 'In honor, yes! First I loved women, then animals. Now I love stones.'

Gringoire is thus part of the transformation or the transition of the meaning of stone. Embodying the succession that Hugo had assigned to the meaning of stone, embodying the succession that Hugo had assigned to the meaning of architecture in CECI TUERA CELA, he can escape the stone-death of the dogmatic, dying world. He is the novel's projection toward the printed word through his profession as "philosopher," that is, scribbler. His association with the printed word establishes the import of his escape from the clutches of the spider king.[7] His escape is no

---

7. The death image of the spider, the web, and the fly has received expert analysis from Richard Grant. See Grant, *The Perilous Quest,* 50–64.

mean feat, and he alone extricates himself from the web of death that ensnares the other characters. In the presence of Louis XI, who initially sees "no objections" to Gringoire's being hanged, our philosopher improvises a brilliant speech that saves his neck. His performance, he would agree, far outranks his early, abortive attempts to stage his mystery play in the novel's opening scene. His plea is buffoonish in appearance—its ostensible purpose and effect are to so demean its author as to make him an unworthy object of the monarch's wrath: "La grande foudre de Dieu ne bombarde pas une laitue" (504) 'God's great lightning bolts don't bombard a head of lettuce.' Yet, his admixture of self-abasement and flattery do not entirely mask a Bakhtinian dialogic slant. When Gringoire begs pity on a poor man who would be harder put to stir up a revolt "than an icicle to strike a spark," we remember that ice can burn, that the printed words of a monk (another "philosopher"?) will soon plunge Europe into turmoil, that the "clownish" character of Gringoire, who here proclaims himself a maker of tragedies and a poet ("Je fais des tragédies. . . . Je suis poète. . . je suis un lettré" 'I write tragedies. . . . I'm a poet . . . a man of letters'), is very close to his Olympian creator writing a novel on the symbiosis of printed word and democracy soon after the revolutionary days of July, 1830.[8]

June, 1830, is the date Hugo gives to "Ce siècle avait deux ans" of *Les Feuilles d'automne*, the poem in which Hugo gives his famous self-definition of "écho sonore." Other poems in the same collection bear witness to his increasing preoccupation with "the people's hour": "Rêverie d'un passant" is dated May 18, 1830, and contains these lines:

> Ecoutez, écoutez, à l'horizon immense,
> Ce bruit qui parfois tombe et soudain recommence,
> Ce murmure confus, ce sourd frémissement
> Qui roule et qui s'accroît de moment en moment.
> C'est le peuple qui vient! c'est la haute marée
> Qui monte incessamment par son astre attirée.

8. This chapter is sprinkled with anachronistic allusions to 1789 and to Hugo's age, such as the discussion concerning the time when "the hour of the people" will come.

> Listen, listen o'er the broad horizon,
> To the noise that falls, then starts anew,
> An indistinct murmuring, a muffled shudder
> That rolls on and grows with every moment.
> The people are coming! The high tide
> Drawn by its star, rises unceasingly.

Other examples include the poem "Pour les pauvres" and, particularly, the closing verses of the last poem, "Amis, un dernier mot!"

> Oh! la muse se doit aux peuples sans défense.
> J'oublie alors l'amour, la famille, l'enfance,
> Et les molles chansons, et le loisir serein.
> Et j'ajoute à ma lyre une corde d'airain!

> Oh! the muse owes herself to defenseless peoples.
> Then I forget love, family, childhood,
> And soft songs, and serene leisure.
> And I add to my lyre a string of brass.

These verses mark an important transition. They look forward to the realization of "la Muse Indignation," that is, the invective of *Châtiments*, and they constitute an important step away from the role of passive consoler assigned to the artist in "Le Poëte dans les révolutions" (*Odes et Ballades*, 1822).

But this far surpasses the possibilities open to Pierre Gringoire. Nevertheless, other artists will inherit a legacy from him. For a Hugo imbued with a passionate commitment to humanitarian reform, the old order must first die and take death away with it: "J'aime la cathédrale et non le moyen âge" 'I love the cathedral and not the Middle Ages' (*Les Quatre Vents de l'esprit*). All Hugo's passion, his scorn and contumely, are poured into the following remarkable passage denouncing the death penalty and flowing in one long and uninterrupted sentence.

C'est une idée consolante, disons-le en passant, de songer que la peine de mort, qui, il y a trois cents ans, encombrait encore de ses roues de fer, de ses gibets de pierre, de tout son attirail de supplices permanent et scellé dans le pavé, la Grève, les Halles, la place Dauphine, la Croix-du-Trahoir, le Marché-aux-Pourceaux, ce hideux Montfaucon, la barrière des Sergents, la Place-aux-Chats, la Porte Saint-Denis, Champeaux, la Porte Baudets, la Porte Saint-Jacques, sans compter les innombrables échelles des prévôts, de l'évêque, des chapitres, des abbés, des prieurs ayant justice; sans compter les noyades juridiques en rivière de Seine; il est consolant qu'aujourd'hui, après avoir perdu sucessivement toutes les pièces de son armure, son luxe de supplice, sa pénalité d'imagination et de fantaisie, sa torture à laquelle elle refaisait tous les cinq ans un lit de cuir au Grand-Châtelet, cette vieille suzeraine de la société féodale, presque mise en place, n'ait plus dans notre immense Paris qu'un coin déshonoré de la Grève, qu'une misérable guillotine, furtive, inquiète, honteuse, qui semble toujours craindre d'être prise en flagrant délit; tant elle disparaît vite après avoir fait son coup! (72–73)

It is a consoling thought, let us state in passing, to think the death penalty, which three hundred years ago still encumbered—with its iron wheels, its stone gibbets, all its torture apparatus permanently embedded in the pavement—the Grève, the Halles, the Place Dauphine, the Croix-du-Trahoir, the Swine Market, the hideous Montfaucon, the Sergeants' barrier, the Place-aux-Chats, the Porte Saint-Denis, Champeaux, the Porte Baudets, the Porte Saint-Jacques, not counting the innumerable pillories of the provost marshals, the Bishop, chapters, abbots and priors dispensing justice, not counting judicial drownings in the river Seine; it is consoling that today, stripped successively of all the pieces of her armor, her refinements of torture, her willful and capricious punishments, her torture, for the administration of which a new leathern bed was made every five years at the Grand Châtelet, that old suzerain of feudal society, nearly outlawed and banished from our cities, hunted from code to code, driven from place to place, should possess in our vast Paris but one ignominious corner of the Grève, but one wretched guillotine—furtive, uneasy, ashamed, which always seems to dread being caught in the act, so quickly does it disappear after having dealt its deadly blow!

The voice that denounces capital punishment—and *Le Dernier Jour d'un condamné* dates from 1829—also announces, however timidly, the entrance of the artist into the arena. Gringoire can preserve life only for himself and for Djali, the artist's talisman that he takes from Esmeralda, but then even Hugo has not quite chased death from the Place de Grève. Far from being the insubstantial character that critics since Ballanche have made him out to be, Pierre Gringoire the fantastic, the *imaginatif*, stands at the center of the novel's emphasis on transition.[9]

9. Simaika, terming Gringoire a "witless puppet . . . who only inspires contempt," approvingly quotes Gustave Planche's nineteenth-century dismissal of our hero as a *caricature grimaçante*: "something more than a household pet, something less than a lackey."

He is Victor Hugo's whimsical self-portrait.[10] His literary progeny, like the printed word, is legion, and *Notre-Dame de Paris* is thus Hugo's portrait of writing as a young art.

Simaika, *L'Inspiration épique,* 54. And according to Patricia Ward, "he serves only a comic purpose." Ward, *The Medievalism of Victor Hugo* (University Park, Pa., 1975), 48. More acutely than she perhaps realizes, she follows this with the comment that "he seems to be a nineteenth-century character wearing medieval costume."

10. Anne Ubersfeld notes two prose fragments in which Hugo designates himself as a grandson of Pierre Gringoire. See Ubersfeld, *Le Roi et le bouffon* (Paris, 1974), 85 n. 52.

III   The Circular Room of George Sand's

Indiana

At the threshold of her novel George Sand is preoccupied by concerns of both moral and realistic order. In her 1832 preface she attempts to justify the moral significance of her work while simultaneously affirming her fidelity to the presentation of a period *tableau de moeurs*. If the "teintes crues et les effets tranchants"[1] 'crude tints and trenchant effects' of the text risk offending the proper reader, she declares, this can be of little concern to the author who has no intention of imposing a grave teaching onto a simple story. Moreover, the author rejects ethical pretentions; she is a humble "diseur, chargé de vous amuser et non de vous instruire" (8) 'storyteller, charged with entertaining, not with instructing you.' And yet, as a "mirror" of reality, a "copying machine" of social data, George Sand puts her faith in the morality inherent in the facts of human existence to exonerate her from any possible reproach of immorality. This faithfulness to the true, she affirms, is far preferable to the scarcely credible (thus hardly moral) artifices of a Marmontel-like tale, an art worthy of the *théâtres du boulevard*. The moral value of *Indiana* will be exemplary: it is better to "servir ses prin-

1. George Sand, *Indiana*, ed. Pierre Salomon (Paris, 1962), 7. All page references in the text are to this edition.

cipes par des exemples vrais que par de poétiques inventions"
(11) 'serve one's principles by means of true examples than poetic inventions.'

These lines have a Stendhalian resonance and evoke the
"roman-miroir" and the "âpre vérité" 'the truth, however harsh,'
of *Le Rouge et le Noir.* They appear to set George Sand's novel
on the level of the social document, whereas "moral" phrases
would instead confine it to the domain of the edifying treatise or
the work of social propaganda.[2] The latter attitude is one that
George Sand will espouse much more openly in the 1842 preface (meanwhile she had written the *Lettres à Marcie* and recently
become the associate of Pierre Leroux in the *Revue Indépendante*),
making the novelist into "le véritable avocat des êtres abstraits
qui représentent nos passions et nos souffrances devant le tribunal de la force et le jury de l'opinion" (17) 'the true advocate
of the abstract beings who represent our passions and our sufferings before the tribunal of superior force and the jury of
public opinion.' Here the comparisons are clear-cut: George
Sand puts society on trial—in particular its injustice toward
women.

Let us compare these two types of novels to consider whether
they exhaust the deep content of *Indiana.* First, the realistic vein,
the Stendhalian or, perhaps even more pertinently, Balzacian *roman de moeurs.* Indeed, Balzac himself had detected in *Indiana*
"une réaction de la vérité contre le fantastique, du temps présent
contre le Moyen Age, du drame intime contre la tyrannie du
genre historique" 'a reaction of the truth against the fantastic,
of present times against the Middle Ages, of personal drama
against the tyranny of the historical genre.'[3]

In *Indiana* there is much evidence of the social, political, and
economic malaise of a France drawing to the difficult end of the
Restoration. There is a querulous province where republicans

2. The word "chronique" 'chronicle,' which recalls the subtitle of *Le Rouge et le Noir,*
occurs in the original edition. See variant *a*, 50. The depiction of "eclectic" salons is
reminiscent of *Armance.*

3. Cited by several authors, notably André Maurois in *Lélia ou la vie de George Sand*
(Paris, 1952), 147.

(Ralph) and Bonapartists (Colonel Delmare) sulk at monarchists (Raymon) and where industrialization is slow to implant itself—the colonel's factory (what it manufactures goes unmentioned, and it will soon go bankrupt) represents a nascent economic reality, still in its infancy in 1827. And there is a Paris that is stifling under the Martignac ministry's Jesuitical atmosphere—*l'escobarderie*—which hangs over the hypocritical and doctrinaire salon of Mme de Carvajal.[4] Class conflicts seem to loom in passages such as the one in which George Sand depicts a society enraged to realize that "la fortune ne résidait plus avec sécurité que chez les plébéiens. . . . Pour se maintenir à la surface du mouvement il fallait être le gendre d'un industriel ou d'un agioteur" (263) 'wealth could no longer be considered secure except in plebeian hands. . . . This class was destined to rise over the ruins of the other, and in order to maintain itself on the surface of the movement, it was necessary to be the son-in-law of a manufacturer or a stock broker.' But this realistic vein is a rather thin one, and with the change of place to the Ile Bourbon the novel appears to turn toward the exotic model. Rather than Stendhal and Balzac, the models now seem to be Rousseau and, above all, Bernardin de Saint-Pierre.

If the significance of *Indiana* is, then, principally one of a socially and personally committed work, must the aesthetic level be abandoned completely, even at the risk of falling into the overexploited and romanticized "life of Lélia"? Must one agree with Henry James (he wrote on at least three occasions of George Sand), who, in phrases whose elegance fails to conceal a certain contempt, seems to see in George Sand and her work only avatars of flamboyant Romanticism and feminist demands: "George Sand is too inveterately moral, too preoccupied with that need to do good which is in art often the enemy of doing well. . . . It is just possible indeed that the moral idea was the real mainspring of her course—I mean a sense of duty of aveng-

---

4. Another tie with Stendhal, since the subtitle of *Armance* is "Quelques scènes d'un salon de Paris en 1827" 'Some Scenes from a Parisian Salon in 1827,' the very year in which *Indiana*'s action begins.

ing on the unscrupulous race of men their immemorial selfish
success with the plastic race of women."[5]

From this viewpoint, it could be claimed that *Indiana* (as well
as *Valentine* and *Lélia*) has returned to favor because of current
events, that is, thanks to the various women's movements. These
novels would then figure as feminist archives, historical docu-
ments of a distressing relevance but also of an outré and picturesque Romanticism. Their interest would be limited to that of a
social plea, the *j'accuse* of the unhappily married woman.

It is to some extent in this spirit that Pierre Salomon, in his
excellent edition of the work, sees *Indiana* first of all as a *roman à
thèse:* "First thesis: woman is unhappy, not only in marriage, but
in love itself. . . . Second thesis: marriage is a detestable in-
stitution" (xiii). And he goes further: "the fundamental theme of
the novel, if it is not the unjust fate of women in marriage, is
unfulfilled love" (xxxiii). But Salomon reaches this conclusion
through the study of certain biographical facts, in particular the
resentment that George Sand allegedly felt toward Aurélien de
Sèze for having respected the Platonic terms of their love agree-
ment. Without dissenting from these conclusions—or even ig-
noring their gender-biased tone—I believe that textual evidence
of a different and more solid nature can be found through the
scrutiny of certain semiotic codes in the novel. These consist,
first, of figurings of illusion—magic enclosures, swirling waters,
and theatrical metaphors—and, second, of mentions of the
chimaera, the monster of myth, the symbol of an ideal that even
Romantic exoticism is incapable of taming: the Ile Bourbon is a
land of exile where the reign of an identical social enslavement
is intact.

More than love that fails to fulfill, it seems to me that it is love
that does not exist—or at least that exists only outside society
(an equally disputable hypothesis, as will be seen in the conclusion)—that is the novel's grand theme. This is of course a Romantic theme par excellence; it characterizes *La Chartreuse de*

5. Henry James, *Notes on Novelists* (New York, 1914), 179.

Parme, but it is also Flaubertian, as in Emma Bovary's "quest" and certainly in the conclusion of *L'Education sentimentale.* In *Indiana* the circular room of the eponymous character articulates this figuration of nothingness; the room seems to draw the presence of all the leading characters. There, one and all discover themselves to be the elect, and ultimately the victims, of amorous illusion.

To a greater extent than Indiana herself, it is no doubt Raymon who will be illusion's chief victim, after having caused its inception in others. From the first, he is identified (by his future wife!) as a "Lovelace," and George Sand herself, in her letter answering Musset's of congratulation, qualifies him as a "pathetic travesty of a Don Juan" (88n). A man of unstable passions, capricious and idle, Raymon amuses himself in political and amorous dalliance, thriving on the presence of danger and the desire for obstacles common to the character of Don Juan. But what is original in this "travesty" of the seducer is that cold-blooded calculations do not always win out over sensibility and that he is thus capable of duping himself. Heir to Constant's *Adolphe,* Raymon de Ramières is moved by his own eloquence, by a gift for elocution that is an integral part of his political talent.

C'était un homme à principes quand il raisonait avec lui-même; mais de fougueuses passions l'entraînaient souvent hors de ses systèmes. Alors il n'était plus capable de réfléchir, ou bien il évitait de se traduire au tribunal de sa conscience: il commettait des fautes comme à l'insu de lui-même, et l'homme de la veille s'efforçait de tromper celui du lendemain. (49)

He was a man of principles when he argued with himself; but strong passions often led him astray from his own theories. Then he became incapable of reasoning, or else he avoided confronting his own conscience: he would err without realizing it, and the man of the night before would try to deceive him of the following day.

En général, et les femmes le savent bien, un homme qui parle d'amour avec esprit est médiocrement amoureux. Raymon était une exception; il exprimait la passion avec art, et il la ressentait avec chaleur. Seulement, ce n'était pas la passion qui le rendait éloquent, *c'était l'éloquence qui le rendait passionné.* Il se sentait du goût pour une femme, et devenait éloquent pour la séduire et amoureux d'elle en la séduisant. (62)

In general, and women are well aware of this, a man who talks wittily of love is not much in love. Raymon was an exception; he could talk of passion artistically and feel it ardently. But it was not passion that made him eloquent, *it was eloquence that made him passionate.* If he had an inclination for a woman, he would become eloquent in order to seduce her, and would fall in love while seducing her.

If Raymon becomes exalted in the midst of pleading his passions, he becomes positively intoxicated with the satisfaction of his senses. Seeking the woman that he had "rêvée. . . la chimère qui m'avait toujours fui" (76) 'dreamt of . . . the chimaera that had always eluded me,' he finds himself in a veritable oneiric delirium—a dream that he mistakes for the ideal. When Noun receives him in Indiana's room, the elements of amorous illusion found there would suffice to deceive many a man less prone to his *chimères* than Raymon. In order to reach the room—a sort of hermetic Venusberg—Raymon traverses a sensual, female night: in the "sinuous" paths the "white fog" drapes the trees in "diaphanous robes" (81). Led by Noun, who can pacify watchdogs, open doors "noiselessly," and guide her lover "in silence," Raymon issues into a circular room, the symbol of a closed and unblemished realm, a perfect, self-sufficient orb, unsullied by external intrusions, a "sanctuaire" of love. This world, self-enfolded and intensified thanks to the play of mirrors that "se renvoyaient . . . l'image de Noun jusqu'à l'infini [et] semblaient se peupler de mille fantômes" (86) 'repeated . . . the image of Noun ad infinitum [and] seemed to be peopled with a thousand phantoms,' and it represents an overflowing of purified sensuality, a Platonic reunion of the body and soul. The intoxicating smells of Indiana's undergarments—a nigh Baudelairean *odor di femina*—are impregnated with balsamic emanations: orange trees, roses, and violets. To the sensual presence of Noun is added the phantom, "le plus pur reflet d'Indiana" 'the purest reflection of Indiana.'[6] The scene is consummated on a

6. That they were conceived as two "halves" is confirmed by the fact that they are "soeurs de lait" 'foster sisters' and that their beauty is complementary: "Noun . . . effaçait de beaucoup par sa beauté resplendissante, la beauté pâle et frêle de madame

bed described as "blanc et pudique comme celui d'une vierge, orné au chevet, en guise de rameau bénit, d'une palme" (82) 'white and modest as a virgin's, and over the headboard, by way of consecrated boxwood, was a bit of palm.' This seraphic Romanticism is illumined by a celestial glow—"transparent" candles and sparkling crystal so bright they had at first dazzled Raymon in his "sudden transition from the darkness to the light." (By contrast with the exaltation of the night, the awakening to "full daylight" will bring only a feeling of dejection and also of "profanation.")

In this scene "Où l'amour cherche en vain d'une main palpitante / Le fantôme adoré de son illusion" 'Where love, with a trembling hand, vainly seeks / The adored phantom of its illusion,' Alfred de Musset fully grasped the merged presences of the ideal and the real; he called Noun "le Réel dans toute sa tristesse" 'the Real in all of its sadness.' And the phantom of Indiana, for him, "N'est-ce pas l'Idéal, cette amour insensée / Qui sur tous les amours plane éternellement?" 'Is she not the Ideal, that mad love / That over all loves forever hovers?" Misfortune inevitably comes to him who would "boire l'idéal dans la réalité!"[7] 'drink the ideal in reality!' Indeed, by morning, when the day has paradoxically dissipated the luminosity of the night, Raymon cannot leave the enclosure from which all the magic has departed; his susceptibility to illusion has left him a prisoner of the real. Locked in the room, he cries out:

—Pourquoi m'avez-vous enfermé ici? lui dit-il enfin. Songez-vous qu'il fait grand jour et que je ne puis sortir sans vous compromettre ouvertement?—Aussi vous ne sortirez pas, lui dit Noun d'un air caressant. La maison est déserte, personne ne peut vous découvrir; le jardinier ne vient jamais dans cette partie du bâtiment, dont seule je garde les clefs. Vous resterez avec moi cette journée encore; vous êtes mon prisonnier. (90)

"Why have you locked me in here?" he said to her at last. "Don't you know that it's broad daylight and that I can't leave without openly compro-

Delamare" (36) 'Noun . . . with her resplendent beauty far outshone Madame Delamare's frail and pallid beauty.'

7. The text of "Après la lecture d'*Indiana*" is printed in the notes to pp. 87–88 of the Salomon edition of *Indiana*. It is also in the "Poésies posthumes" of Musset's *Poésies Nouvelles*, ed. M. Allem (Paris, 1958), 247–48.

mising you?" "And so you won't leave," Noun told him caressingly. "The house is deserted and no one can discover you; the gardener never comes to this part of the building, to which I alone have the keys. You will stay with me all day long; you are my prisoner."

So Raymon becomes the prisoner of love; the old concetto is renewed, but not the way he might wish it. The revenge of the real here presages the reality that awaits him at the end of the novel in the person of Laure de Nangy, the young heiress who will become his wife by dispassionately negotiating a *mariage de raison* with him.

Elle mettait tout son orgueil à n'être point au-dessous de ce siècle froid et raisonneur; son amour-propre eût souffert d'y porter les niaises illusions d'une pensionnaire ignorante; elle eût rougi d'une déception comme d'une sottise; elle faisait, en un mot, consister son héroïsme à échapper à l'amour, comme madame Delamare mettait le sien à s'y livrer. . . . Pour elle, la vie était un calcul stoïque, et le bonheur une illusion puérile, dont il fallait se défendre comme d'une faiblesse et d'un ridicule. (293–94)

She made it a matter of self-esteem not to be unworthy of the cold and scheming times; her pride would have suffered had she fallen victim to the silly illusions of an ignorant boarding-school girl; she would have blushed at being deceived as at being caught doing something foolish; in a word, her heroism consisted in avoiding love, just as Madame Delamare's consisted in giving herself over to it. . . . For her, life was a stoic calculation, and happiness a childish illusion, something to guard oneself against as a weakness and an absurdity.

Even before their marriage, Laure de Nangy seems to enjoy depicting the fragility of his illusions to Raymon. This occurs quite explicitly when he finds her making watercolor copies of some odd wainscoting pictures with stilted figures: "elle avait saisi l'esprit faux et chatoyant du siècle de Louis XV" (288) 'she had grasped the false and shifting character of the century of Louis XV.' The paneling is covered with rustic love scenes, that is, scenes of ideal, pastoral love that Raymon has sought to enact. Laure delights in mocking their artificiality.

Et cette jolie nature fausse et peignée, ces buissons de rose à cent feuilles au milieu des bois, où de nos jours ne croissent plus que des haies d'églantiers, ces oiseaux apprivoisés dont l'espèce a disparu apparemment, ces robes de satin rose que le soleil ne ternissait pas . . . ridicules fictions (289)

And that pretty landscape, so false and groomed, those thousand-petaled rosebushes in the midst of the woods, where, in our time, only eglantine grows, those tame birds of a species that seems to have disappeared, those pink satin gowns that the sun never faded . . . absurd fictions.

As for the circular room, we may note that the subject of slavery is added to the scene not as a veneer of concern or a contrived denouement, but rather as an integral part of George Sand's sorrowful vision of love, irrespective of her feminist program. At the height of that "purely Oriental lust" (for "Oriental" read "Creole"), the author slips in the following observation: "Si madame Delamare n'eût eu, pour l'embellir, son esclavage et ses souffrances, Noun l'eût infiniment surpassée en beauté dans cet instant; elle était splendide de douleur et d'amour" (85) 'If, to increase her charms Madame Delamare had not had her slavery and her sufferings, Noun would have surpassed her in beauty in that moment; she was resplendent in her grief and her love.' In Part Four of the novel this aesthetics of dolorism will be enriched with the theme of exile. Expelled from her country and her home, Indiana in turn seeks entry to the magic room. (In this rather too facile "ironic" reversal, Raymon has become the owner of Le Lagny and the occupant of the circular room.) The vocabulary is the same, as is the desperate attempt to settle into the love illusion: "En mettant pied sur une terre qui appartenait à Raymon et qui allait devenir son asile, son *sanctuaire*, sa forteresse et sa patrie, elle sentit son coeur bondir de joie" (299) 'Setting foot on land that belonged to Raymon and was to become her asylum, her *sanctuary*, her fortress and her homeland, she felt her heart leap for joy.' Rushing into the room, where she finds Raymon alone, she bursts out: "Reconnais-moi donc, s'écria-t-elle; c'est moi, c'est ton Indiana, c'est ton *esclave* que tu as rappelée de l'*exil* et qui est venue de trois mille lieues pour t'aimer et te servir" (300, italics added) 'Speak to me,' she cried; 'it is I, your Indiana, your *slave* whom you recalled from *exile* and who has traveled three thousand leagues to love you and to serve you.'

But just before Raymon can lock the door (as if to capture the love illusion and enslave it), Laure de Nangy, Indiana's antithesis, the incarnation of destructive reality, breaks up this moment, with its stuff of the *scène à faire*. She underscores its artificiality by her use of theatrical metaphors,[8] saying: "Madame Delamare, vous vous plaisez, ce me semble, à mettre trois personnages dans une étrange situation; mais je vous remercie de m'avoir donné le rôle le moins ridicule, et voici comme je m'en acquitte. Veuillez vous retirer" (302) 'Madame Delamare, you seem to enjoy placing three persons in an awkward situation; but I do thank you for assigning me the least ridiculous role, and here is how I discharge it. Be so good as to withdraw.' And the drama becomes vaudeville, even a touch Pirandellian for the modern reader: "Je vous laisse le soin de terminer cette scène absurde" 'I'll leave it to you to finish this absurd scene.'

The privileged place of the vaporous idyll, the circular form of the dream chamber overtly evokes the exotic existence of the Ile Bourbon, of which it is simultaneously the presage and the condensed expression. There is no point in rehearsing its luminous, tropical intensity and its odiferous delights—such as the "aromatic infusion of the *faham*." Its contents are also significant. The "chaste" simplicity of the furnishings alludes to that of the hut and the "chaumière indienne" 'the Indian cottage'; its books of love and travel project us through space to the conical island paradise. But above all, its walls are decorated with engravings representing "les pastorales amours de Paul et Virginie, les cimes de l'Ile Bourbon et les rivages bleus de Saint-Paul" (82) 'the pastoral love of Paul and Virginia, the peaks of the Ile Bourbon and the blue shores of Saint-Paul.' The last element is the portrait of Ralph, which Raymon unveils to great wrath and jealousy: "Et quoi! se dit-il, cet Anglais . . . a le privilège d'être admis dans l'appartement le plus secret de madame Delamare! Son insipide image est toujours là qui regarde froidement les actes les plus intimes de sa vie! Il la surveille, il la garde, il suit tous ses mouvements, il la possède à toute heure!" (92) 'What! he said to himself, this Englishman . . . enjoys

8. Nicole Bothorel, "L'Obstacle romanesque dans quelques oeuvres de George Sand," *Etudes Littéraires*, III (1970), 65–75, cites the obstacle/opposition between "Théâtre et Réalité" in *La Marquise*.

the privilege of being admitted to the innermost apartment of Madame Delamare! His insipid face is always here looking coldly on the most private acts of her life! He watches her, guards her, follows her every movement, possesses her every hour of the day!' Such will indeed be the exact privileges and duties of Ralph on the Ile Bourbon.

Thus, the Ile Bourbon, the harmonic reciprocal of the circular room, is also a place of illusion. Upon her return there from her native land, Indiana lives solely on mirages. In the course of her solitary walks "il lui semblait qu'au-delà de ces vagues et de ces brumes lointaines la magique apparition d'une autre terre allait se révéler à ses regards" (249) 'it seemed to her that beyond those waves and that distant haze, the magical apparition of another land was about to reveal itself to her eyes.' Indiana's mind strays into the "illusions of the past," and she comes close to madness. Yet, she could not have continued to live without these aberrations, "car, chez elle, tout se rapportait à une certaine faculté d'illusions" (250) 'for in her case, everything centered on a certain capacity for creating illusions.' So Indiana feasts on empty horizons, desperately seeking in them the satisfaction of her illusions: "Elle vécut ainsi des semaines et des mois sous le ciel des tropiques, n'aimant, ne connaissant, ne caressant qu'une ombre, ne creusant qu'une chimère" (250) 'Thus she lived for weeks and months under the tropical sky, loving, recognizing, caressing what was only a shade, contemplating what was only a chimaera.'

It is worth noting, insofar as the theme of exile is concerned, that the Biblical sources of *Indiana* play a rather important role. We know from a letter written by George Sand to Emile Regnault (February 28, 1832) that her character first bore the name Noémi. George Sand here was thinking of the widow followed to Judea by her daughter-in-law Ruth (a Moabite) after her husband's death. There Ruth the stranger will marry Boaz, Naomi's relative, a man much older than Ruth. George Sand assigns Ralph, Indiana's cousin ten years older than she, the role of Boaz and fuses the two characters of Ruth and Naomi in order to arrive at the amorous complexity of Indiana. George

Sand was to make much of foreign lands, departures, and exiles.[9]

If the Ile Bourbon and the magic room, idyllic circular spaces where the characters vainly seek to live within their illusions, are equivalent on the level of the thematics of love, there is one element—water—that links them and imparts to them the feeling of despair that suffuses the novel (at least before the reader comes to the factitious denouement that George Sand gave—or was forced to give—to her work). This is not the saline water of the ocean—a purely mimetic aspect of the novel—but the fresh waters of the rivers that course through Le Lagny and the Ile Bourbon and that acquire a moral significance conferred upon them by a whole series of images in *Indiana*. There is, first, Noun's rather Shakespearean suicide, her drowning in the waters of the small stream that crosses the property of Le Lagny.[10] This is a "model" suicide in a sense, for Indiana twice attempts to imitate it, by throwing herself first into the Seine, then (in Ralph's arms) from the top of Bernica. The explanation she offers is, "J'ai toujours été attirée vers le bord des eaux par une sympathie invincible, par le souvenir de ma pauvre Noun" (313) 'I have always been drawn to the water's edge by an irresistible sympathy, by the memory of my poor Noun.' Water is then semiotically coded as despair and marked by the failures of love so feared by the characters—and of course by death itself. Indiana's married name, *Del-mare* points to her inclination to this fate and brings marriage within the same ambit of illusion and death. Finally, let us briefly recall the dog, which is named Ophelia and which accompanies nearly all these scenes; Indiana will see her corpse floating on the water, her skull split open by blows from the oars.

The attraction to water is George Sand's. In *Histoire de ma vie* she wrote: "C'était l'eau surtout qui m'attirait comme par un charme mystérieux. . . . Arrêtée sur le bord et comme en-

---

9. Paul Berret, in his edition of *La Légende des siècles* (Paris, 1921), I, 81, noted that from 1822 to 1859, the date of "Booz endormi," the book of Ruth inspired ten artistic and literary works.

10. Compare *Lélia*, in which Sténio commits suicide in a lake.

chaînée par un aimant, je sentais dans ma tête comme une gaieté fébrile en me disant: Comme c'est aisé! Je n'aurais qu'un pas à faire"[11] 'It was water in particular that attracted me like a mysterious charm. . . . Halted on the edge and held as if by a magnet, I felt a feverish gaiety in my head and thought: How easy! I'd only have to take a step.'

But what of the denouement of *Indiana?* In it we can find certain thematic elements well established in the narrative: Boaz-Ralph will be united (but not in marriage) to Ruth-Indiana, and they will use their income to buy the freedom of slaves, lamenting that they are not rich enough to "deliver all those living in slavery." The solitude of the couple is even envisaged as a compensation for the social ostracism they suffer, as a victory over exile. But the obvious subterfuge by which they elude death—death that had been marked as their destiny, their suicide by drowning—is a *faux-fuyant*, an evasion. The deep lesson of *Indiana* is instead the impossibility of installing oneself in an illusion of amorous felicity—and not the exotic evasion and contentment of the closing words: "retournez au monde; si quelque jour il vous bannit, souvenez vous de notre chaumière indienne" 'return to society; if it banishes you someday, remember our Indian cottage.' This artificial ending would seem to lend credence to the tradition according to which George Sand, "who disliked tragic endings, changed her mind and added an epilogue in which Indiana and Ralph, as they are about to leap into the abyss suddenly discover, she that she is capable of loving again, and he that he has always loved her."[12] Another hypothesis is the more material one of the novel's editor, Pierre Salomon, who posits a publisher in need of some additional pages to flesh out the second volume of the popular two-volume novel format.

Both hypotheses are supported by the observation that the chain of key images suddenly loses its harmonic components. The love dream always dissipates; never can the chimaera be ensnared. The circular room, like some unreachable, impalpable

11. George Sand, *Histoire de ma vie* (4 vols., Paris, 1879), IV, Ch. 6.
12. W. Karénine, *George Sand: Sa vie et ses oeuvres* (Paris, 1899), I, 370.

Cythaera, is the symbol of a perfection that mocks the human and pushes it, out of despair of ever attaining it, toward suicide. Suicide thus becomes homage, a gesture of perfectionism, and an attempt to regain the exaltation of sphericity. In *Indiana* the characters' very vocation beckons them toward death.

IV 🕷 The Grand Illusion: Vigny's

Servitude et Grandeur militaires

At the end of 1835 Vigny described *Servitude et Grandeur militaires* as forming one of the cantos of "une sorte de poème épique sur la désillusion" 'a sort of epic poem about disillusionment.' And more precisely, a little more than a year later, he characterized his novel as an "oraison funèbre de l'armée de la Restauration"[1] 'a funeral oration for the army of the Restoration.' The book is the fruit of several conjugated concerns, which are personal, historical, and literary. The historical impulsions in the creation of *Servitude* are as important as any, for the role of political police, forced upon the French army between 1830 and 1835, was a degradation to which Vigny reacted strongly. In these years the army was called upon to put down revolts in the provinces (and in the capital) such as those touched off in 1831, and again in 1834, by the Lyon silk weavers' descent from the misery of their Croixrousse stronghold.

> Pour gouverner il faut avoir
> Manteaux ou rubans en sautoir (bis).

1. Alfred de Vigny, *Le Journal d'un poète*, in Vigny, *Œuvres complètes*, ed. F. Baldensperger (2 vols.; Paris, 1948), II, 1037, 1053. The other two cantos (for Vigny's imagination is characteristically triangular) are *Stello* and *Cinq-Mars*.

Nous en tissons pour vous, grands de la terre,
Et nous, pauvres canuts, sans drap on nous enterre.
 C'est nous les canuts
 Nous sommes tout nus (bis).
Mais quand notre règne arrive
Quand votre règne finira,
Alors nous tisserons le linceul du vieux monde
Car on entend déjà la révolte qui gronde.
 C'est nous les canuts
 Nous n'irons plus tout nus.[2]

To rule requires
Death-crossed cloaks and ribbons.
We weave them for you, ye great of this earth,
And we poor *canuts* (silk weavers) are buried without cloth.
 We are the *canuts*
 We are naked.
But when our reign shall come
When yours shall end,
Then shall we weave the old world's shroud
For already the stirring of revolt can be heard.
 We are the *canuts*
 We shall no longer go about unclothed.

The *canuts* were firmly repressed by the intervention of the army, but the fear that the bourgeoisie felt at these stirrings of laboring, therefore endangering, classes dwelt on.[3] It is fairly expressed in this speech of 1831 by Saint-Marc Girardin, defender of property rights against the new "barbarians."

Il faut que la classe moyenne sache bien quel est l'état des choses; il faut qu'elle connaisse bien sa condition. Elle a au-dessous d'elle une population de prolétaires qui s'agite et frémit sans savoir ce qu'elle veut, sans savoir où elle ira. Que lui importe? elle est mal: elle veut changer. Là est le danger de la société moderne; de là peuvent sortir les Barbares qui la détruiraient. Dans cet état des choses, il est nécessaire que la classe moyenne comprenne bien ses intérêts et le devoir qu'elle a à remplir. . . . [Elle] serait dupe si . . . elle donnait follement des armes et des droits à ses ennemis, si elle laissait entrer le flot des prolétaires dans la garde nationale,

2. Quoted in Eric J. Hobsbawn, *The Age of Revolution, 1789–1848* (Cleveland, 1962), 200.
3. See Louis Chevalier, *Classes laborieuses et classes dangereuses à Paris pendant la première moitié du XIXe siècle* (Paris, 1958).

dans les institutions municipales, dans les lois électorales, dans tout ce qui est l'Etat. Il serait bien temps vraiment de vouloir repousser l'ennemi après l'avoir reçu dans la place. Il ne s'agit ici ni de république ni de monarchie: il s'agit du salut de la société.[4]

The middle class must fully know the situation; it must grasp its condition. Below it, it has a population of proletarians, restive and simmering, unaware of its desires or aims. What do they care? They are hurting; they want to change. There lies the danger for modern society; thence can issue the Barbarians who would destroy it. In this state of affairs, it is necessary for the middle class to understand fully its interests and the duty it has to fulfull. . . . It would be mistaken if it madly gave arms and rights to its enemies, if it allowed the horde of proletarians to enter the national guard, municipal institutions, electoral processes, everything that pertains to government. It is high time to repel the enemy after having received it in the bastion. This is not a question of a republic or a monarchy: it concerns the safety of society.

With less pompous concern for society's preservation, Lucien Leuwen, Stendhalian veteran of the "potato wars," expressed his simple disgust for soldiering in the period.

Je ne veux plus de l'état militaire en temps de paix, c'est-à-dire: passer ma soirée à jouer au billard et à m'eniver au café, et encore avec défense de prendre sur la table de marbre mal essuyée d'autre journal que le *Journal de Paris*. Dès que nous sommes trois officiers à [nous] promener ensemble, un au moins peut passer pour espion dans l'esprit des deux autres. Le colonel, autrefois intrépide soldat, s'est transformé, sous la baguette du juste milieu, en sale commissaire de police.[5]

I don't want anything more to do with the military in peacetime, that is, spending my evening playing billiards and getting drunk in the café, and even then being forbidden to look at any newspaper lying on the dirty marble tables except the *Journal de Paris*. As soon as three of us officers start taking a walk together, at least one can be suspected as a spy by the other two. The colonel, who once was a daring soldier, has been changed into a dirty police commissioner by the wand of *juste milieu* policies.

4. Saint-Marc Girardin, *Souvenirs et réflexions politiques d'un journaliste* (Paris, 1859), 148–49.

5. Stendhal, *Lucien Leuwen*, in Stendhal, *Romans et nouvelles*, ed. H. Martineau (2 vols.; Paris, 1952), I, 1070–71. The phrase *juste milieu*, so derisively voiced in *Lucien Leuwen* (by the Henricinquistes, of course), was the political slogan of the July Monarchy and was apparently launched by Louis-Philippe himself in an address to the town of Gaillac in January, 1831): "We seek a position right in the middle [*le juste milieu*] equidistant from the excesses of popular rule and the abuses of royal rule."

The most appalling incident in these years of social strife came about in Paris (hard on the heels of renewed rioting in Lyon) on April 14, 1834, when the military butchered many of the inhabitants of a building on the rue Transnonain. Daumier's famous lithograph has enshrined the incident in revolutionary and antimilitaristic iconology.

The degradation of the army was all the more disturbing to Vigny's generation in that it made for disillusioning contrasts with the propagandizing of the Napoleonic legend that got under way around 1832. That year marked the death of the Roi de Rome, and the following year Napoleon's statue was replaced on top of the Vendôme column. In 1840 the emperor's ashes were returned to France and translated in great pomp to the Invalides. The Orleanist regime, itself sadly lacking in military prestige, obviously hoped that some of the glamour of the Empire would devolve upon it, and so little did it fear Bonapartism that it actively encouraged the legend.

Such events evoked memories of schoolboy enthusiasm for the military feats of the Empire, such as those described in *La Confession d'un enfant du siècle* or, for Vigny, in the introductory chapter of *Servitude et Grandeur militaires:* "Les maîtres mêmes ne cessaient de nous lire les bulletins de la Grand Armée, et nos cris de Vive l'Empereur! interrompaient Tacite et Platon. Nos précepteurs ressemblaient à des hérauts d'armes, nos salles d'études à des casernes, nos récréations à des manoeuvres, et nos examens à des revues"[6] 'The masters themselves never stopped reading us the bulletins of the Grande Armée, and our shouts of Vive l'Empereur! interrupted Tacitus and Plato. Our preceptors seemed like military heralds, our study halls like barracks, our recreations like field maneuvers, and our exams like military parades.'

Yet Vigny's military career was unhappy and unsuccessful. As he himself explains, "J'avais porté dans une vie tout active une nature toute contemplative" (15) 'To a wholly active life I had brought a wholly contemplative nature.' Moreover, as he

6. Alfred de Vigny, *Servitude et Grandeur militaires*, ed. F. Germain (Paris, 1965), 14. All page references in the text are to this edition.

writes in his *Journal*, "La Destinée m'a refusé la guerre que j'aimais; j'ai fait *Servitude et Grandeur militaires* avec le désir de hâter la destruction de l'amour de la gloire guerrière que je n'ai pu conquérir"[7] 'Fate denied me war, which I loved; I composed *Servitude et Grandeur militaires* with the desire of hastening the destruction of the love of martial glory that I was unable to subdue.' Vigny, therefore, felt a great gulf between garrison life and dreams of Napoleonic glory, between the passive obedience of a military code and his own highly independent character.

To these personal reasons we must join literary ones, for *Servitude* is merely one in a series of books devoted to the outcasts of modern society: the *gentilhomme* (*Cinq-Mars*, 1826), the poet (*Stello*, 1832), the soldier (*Servitude*, 1835), and the religious thinker (*Daphné*, 1837). *Servitude* is specifically a continuation of *Stello*, inasmuch as it, too, is a kind of "consultation": whereas earlier the Docteur Noir had prescribed skepticism in political matters, now Vigny himself undertakes to dispel another set of illusions. As Gaëtan Picon put it, "To dream of heroism is as chimerical as dreaming of a social mission for the poet."[8]

Perhaps most powerful of all literary impulsions in the genesis of the novel was Vigny's reading of Joseph de Maistre's *Soirées de Saint-Pétersbourg* in 1832. In his introduction to *Servitude*, François Germain has fully documented the extent of Maistre's influence, or counterinfluence, on the composition of the book. The soldier, according to Maistre, slaughters innocents, but in doing so, he is carrying out the orders of a monarch whose inspiration is divine. He is, therefore, an incarnation of supernatural grandeur, a *bourreau divin*, a divine executioner (xxii). Vigny's own horror of killing, intensified by contemporary events and by his reading—of Joseph de Maistre, for example, but also of other social and religious thinkers, such as Lamennais, Buchez, and Ballanche—comes squarely into conflict with his admiration for voluntary sacrifice. *Servitude et Grandeur militaires* attempts to resolve this antinomy. Germain is

7. Vigny, *Journal*, II, 1050.
8. Gaëtan Picon, "Le Roman et la prose lyrique au XIXe siècle," in *Histoire des littératures*, Encyclopédie de la Pléiade (Paris, 1958), III, 1023.

right to suggest that the book is a work of personal dialectic: "the opposing convictions that the army is admirable for its sacrifice but odious for its killing are reconciled in this way: the army is admirable because it submits to the duty, odious in its view, of killing" (xxiv). It is important to note, however, that the resolution of the problem is achieved without recourse to external or metaphysical principles of justification. Indeed, its achievement is perhaps realized *because of* this absence of adequate guidance through authority.

Resolution is not equally realized in each of the three tales that make up *Servitude et Grandeur militaires*. To take the first tale, "Laurette ou le cachet rouge" 'Laurette; or, the Red Seal,' it is clear that the ship's captain obeys the Directoire's orders reluctantly, but he does obey them instantly and has his young friend shot without hesitation.[9] The captain compares himself to a *mécanique* (machine) that blindly obeys, and does not blame his profession itself for his "adventure."

—Je comprends bien, lui dis-je, comme s'il eût fini son histoire, qu'après une aventure aussi cruelle on prenne son métier en horreur.

—Oh! le métier, êtes-vous fou? me dit-il brusquement, ce n'est pas le métier! Jamais le capitaine d'un bâtiment ne sera obligé d'être un bourreau, sinon quand viendront des gouvernements d'assassins et de voleurs, qui profiteront de l'habitude qu'a un pauvre homme d'obéir aveuglément, d'obéir toujours, d'obéir comme une malheureuse mécanique, malgré son cœur. (53)

"I can understand," said I as if he had finished his story, "that after such a cruel experience anyone would become horrified by his profession!"

"The profession! Are you mad?" he replied at once. "It isn't the profession! Never will a ship captain be obliged to become an executioner unless we get governments of killers and thieves, who will take advantage of a poor man's habit of obeying blindly, of obeying at all times, of obeying like a miserable automaton, in spite of his heart."

This passage translates, in terms of the fiction, Vigny's contention in the introductory pages of the book that "l'Armée est aveugle et muette. Elle frappe devant elle du lieu où on la met.

9. The source of this tale provides an excellent practical example of the theory of "Vérité dans l'Art," which Vigny expounded in the preface to *Cinq-Mars*. See *Servitude*, xxvii–xxviii.

Elle ne veut rien et agit par ressort. C'est une grande chose que l'on meut et qui tue; mais aussi c'est une chose qui souffre" (21) 'the army is blind and dumb. Set it down, and it strikes out. It has no will of its own and acts like a spring. It is a grand thing that is set in motion and kills; but it is also a thing that can suffer.' This is also in line with the book's epigraph—*Ave, Caesar, morituri te salutant*—which clearly indicates Vigny's preoccupation with the Caesarism that transforms the soldier into a gladiator who kills and dies without reason, spectacularly. Curiously enough, however, the story itself serves to expose the insufficiencies of *dévouement, sacrifice,* and *abnégation* (21, 24), which in his introduction Vigny had singled out as particularly redemptive and elevating qualities of the military career.

Let us take the protagonist of "Laurette." It is surprising that the captain, who so swiftly obeys his execution orders (like the *mécanique* he mentions) feels no "remorse for [his] obedience" (62), indeed, seems hardly to suffer from his act. Germain wonders if the novella, given this absence of remorse, really does pose a *cas de conscience* (xxxi): if the captain has given up the sea, he continues to pursue his military career on land. Vigny's intention here, however, seems to have been the illustration of another thesis. He writes, toward the end of "Laurette," that the gruff exterior of the soldier nearly always conceals a deep sensibility: "—La dureté l'homme de guerre est comme un masque de fer sur un noble visage, comme un cachot de pierre qui renferme un prisonnier royal" (55) 'The soldier's harshness is like an iron mask on a noble visage, like a stone prison enclosing a royal prisoner.'[10] The real significance of this analogy is not made wholly clear in "Laurette," but in the following tale, "La Veillée de Vincennes," we come upon this passage:

Les choses se passent ainsi dans une société d'où la sensibilité est retranchée. C'est un des côtés mauvais du métier des armes que cet excès de force où l'on prétend toujours guinder son caractère. On s'exerce à durcir son coeur, on se cache de la pitié, de peur qu'elle ne ressemble à la faiblesse; on se fait effort pour dissimuler le sentiment divin de la compas-

10. The allusion is to Vigny's early poem "La Prison"; the link is the theme of undeserved destiny.

sion, *sans songer qu'à force d'enfermer un bon sentiment on étouffe le prisonnier.* (121; italics added)

This is what happens in a society where sensitivity is repressed. One of the bad sides of the military profession is this excessive force that is always applied to the repression of one's character. One practices hardening one's heart, one hides from pity, lest it appear to be weakness; one strives to conceal the divine feeling of compassion, *without considering that by dint of locking up a good feeling one stifles the prisoner.* (italics added)

The conclusion here is obvious: by stifling one's feelings, one becomes a monster of indifference. We may also conclude that devotion, sacrifice, and abnegation will not prevent one from becoming such a monster.

This is an apparently puzzling train of arguments, for the denigration of these soldierly qualities constitutes a discrediting of the book's initial thesis. Yet, if there is confusion here, there is nothing perverse in it. It is true that at the conclusion of "La Veillée de Vincennes," with its rejection of *dévouement*, the reader feels oddly baffled (if not cheated) and may assume that the book has been poorly thought out. Still, this is only partially true, for *Servitude et Grandeur militaires* is a work in gestation, a book still being thought out as the reader comes to the last of its three stories, "La Vie et la mort du capitaine Renaud ou la Canne de jonc" 'The Life and Death of Captain Renaud; or, The Malacca Cane.'[11]

"La Canne de jonc" is consequently by far the most important section of the book. In it Vigny's moral and artistic concerns cohere at last. The story is also the most successful of *Servitude* and fittingly caps the work.[12] This story goes beyond the partisan passions of the 1830s. Vigny is not concerned here with disproving Maistre's sanctification of massacre or refuting

11. Progressively layered or tiered composition is characteristic of Vigny's art. It is not by chance that the passage most illustrative of this process should be found precisely in the last pages of *Servitude*. See the passage quoted below on p. 56. See also the history of *Servitude*'s publication in installments and my "Notes on Vigny's Composition," *Modern Language Review*, LX (1965), 369–75.

12. Thus, François Germain writes that "La Canne de jonc" stands as a virtual *summum*, so many certainties does it offer (p. lvi). And according to James Doolittle, it is "the best piece of prose to come from Vigny's pen." Doolittle, *Alfred de Vigny* (New York, 1967), 199.

Lamennais' negation (in *Paroles d'un croyant*) of military grandeur.[13] Rather Vigny goes so far as to condemn the very nature of war: "C'est la guerre qui a tort et non pas nous" (210) 'It is war that is wrong, not us,' says Captain Renaud, for war signifies the enslavement of conscience. The problem of the soldier-gladiator poses one of those supremely agonizing dilemmas that in Vigny admit only of human resolution. For Joseph de Maistre and for Lamennais, the problem of the soldier was social, political, and divine. For Vigny, it is a human problem. This is why, in the conclusion of "La Canne de jonc," Vigny vaunts honor as the soldier's redemptive virtue.

Tandis que toutes les vertus semblent descendre du ciel pour nous donner la main et nous élever, celle-ci paraît venir de nous-mêmes et tendre à monter jusqu'au ciel. —C'est une vertu *tout humaine* que l'on peut croire *née de la terre* sans palme céleste après la mort; c'est la vertu de la vie. (216; italics added)

While all the other virtues seem to descend from Heaven to extend us their hand and raise us up, this virtue seems to come from within us and to move heavenwards. —It is a *completely human* virtue that we can believe *born of the earth* and earning no celestial reward after death; it is the virtue of life. (italics added)

Similar confrontations between the human and the natural or the supernatural in Vigny's poetry characteristically end with combative, Pascalian affirmations of man's dignity and grandeur in his knowledge of defeat: his declaration "J'aime la majesté des souffrances humaines" 'I love the majesty of human sufferings' ("La Maison du berger") is the most famous instance of this

13. In Chapter 35 of *Paroles d'un croyant* Satan says to the tyrants: "Prenez dans chaque famille les jeunes gents les plus robustes, et donnez-leur des armes, et exercez-les à les manier, et ils combattront pour vous contre leurs pères et leurs frères; car je leur persuaderai que c'est une action glorieuse. Je leur ferai deux idoles, et ils se soumettront à cette loi aveuglément, parce que je séduirai leur esprit, et vous n'aurez plus rien à craindre" 'From every family take the strongest young men, give them weapons, and train them in their use, and they shall fight on your behalf against their fathers and brothers; for I shall convince them that this is a glorious action. I shall make two idols for them, and they shall blindly submit to this law, because I shall seduce their minds, and you shall have nothing more to fear.' Félicité Robert de Lamennais, *Œuvres complètes* (10 vols.; Paris, 1844), X, 115. The importance of this passage for *Servitude* was first noted by Marc Citoleux, *Alfred de Vigny, persistances classiques et affinités étrangères* (Paris, 1924), 7–10.

mood. There is also the notion of metaphysical revolt, as instanced in the *strophe du silence* ("Le Mont des oliviers"), of which more later.

Honor, then, is presented as the only virtue emanating from man. It is called "la conscience, mais la conscience exaltée" (217) 'conscience, but in a heightened form,' and also "la pudeur virile" (218) 'manly modesty,' vague definitions that strike us as excessively abstract. Honor, as "La Canne de jonc" shows us, must be assimilated through the immediacy of individual human experience. Honor is not a lesson that can be taught, not a wisdom transmissible from generation to generation, from father to son. In "La Canne de jonc" the formation of Renaud's conscience is achieved through a series of lessons, three in number, that are intended to illustrate Vigny's contention that experience alone is operative in matters of high moral concern: "Il en est ainsi presque toujours de tous les conseils écrits ou parlés. L'expérience seule et le raisonnement qui sort de nos propres réflexions peuvent nous instruire" (180) 'It's almost always this way with all written or spoken advice. Only experience and reasoning that comes from our own considerations can teach us anything.' This passage is essential to an understanding of the structure of "La Canne de jonc," for the story itself follows a narrative strand of three such lessons of written advice, spoken advice, and experience.

Written advice comes first, with a letter of paternal advice addressed to Renaud by his father, when the latter was a prisoner of war, wherein the son's excessive adulation of Bonaparte, his "Séidisme," is denounced. Vigny, as author-narrator, has acquired this letter and often rereads it "pour bien me convaincre de l'inutilité des avis que donne une génération à celle qui la suit, et réfléchir sur l'absurde entêtement des mes illusions" (144) 'fully to persuade myself of the futility of the advice one generation hands down to the next, and to ponder the absurd obstinacy of my illusions.' "Séidisme," the fictional embodiment of Vigny's dreams of military glory, takes the form of Renaud's youthful admiration of Bonaparte, an enthusiasm "qui fut le but et la folie de ma vie" (140) 'that was my life's goal and folly' and that leads him to become one of the emperor's pages. While performing these duties, he receives his father's letter, with its description of Bonaparte as a charlatan, an epithet that prepares the famous scene in which the pope responds to the emperor's alternating cajolery and bluster by a disdainful "*Commediante!*" and "*Tragediante!*" Renaud, trapped in an alcove, unintentionally witnesses this extraordinary scene; he is impressed by the pope's dignity and appalled by the baseness of Napoleon's ambition. Napoleon is even seen to agree with the pope's judgment: "—C'est vrai! Tragédien ou Comédien. — Tout est rôle, tout est costume pour moi depuis longtemps et pour toujours. Quelle fatigue! quelle petitesse! Poser! toujours poser! . . . —Moi, il faut que j'aille et que je fasse aller" (164) 'It's true. Tragic or comic actor, everything is playacting, dressing up, as far as I am concerned—for a long time now. How tiresome! how petty! Posing, always posing! . . . I have to stay in motion, and make others do the same.' Thus, even the man of action is ensnared in make-believe and illusion.

Thus, Renaud's subsequent assignment to sea duty comes as a relief. His first lesson against war has taken place, but as he tells us, he is unmindful of its significance: "—Cependant ce fut plutôt l'idée gigantesque de la guerre qui désormais m'apparut, que celle de l'homme qui la représentait d'une si redoutable façon, et je sentis à cette grande vue un enivrement insensé redoubler en moi pour la gloire des combats, m'étourdissant sur le maître qui les ordonnait" (169) 'And yet from that time on it was rather the grand concept of war that occupied me, rather than the man who symbolized it so impressively, and at this grandiose vision I felt redoubling in me a mad intoxication for the glories of the battle, blinding me as to the master who ordered it.'

The second lesson, one of spoken advice, is immediately at hand. On Renaud's first day at sea, off the abandoned invasion port at Boulogne, his ship is rammed and sunk, and Renaud becomes a prisoner of the English. It is not by chance that he should be, like his father before him, the prisoner of Admiral Collingwood. Both men stand in a paternal relationship to

Renaud, and both men are *absent* fathers. Most important, both men offer advice that remains abstract and ineffectual until personalized by experience. Collingwood's lesson for Renaud is one of honor through devotion to duty and country. Thanks to such abnegation, Collingwood is able to bear the loneliness of long years at sea. In Collingwood's acceptance of his isolation there is a Roman simplicity that arouses Renaud's sympathy. And Collingwood's advice to devote himself to a principle rather than to a man (189) seems wise, particularly upon Renaud's liberation (thanks to an exchange) and return to Paris, where he is scorned by Napoleon: "—Je n'aime pas les prisonniers, dit-il; on se fait tuer" (192) '"I don't like prisoners," he said; "one tries to be killed."'

Renaud throws himself into the infantry, seeking no distinction but that of obscurely serving France. Renaud believes that in this way he is serving his country, as Collingwood had urged, avenging himself on Bonaparte by doing his patriotic duty without depending on Napoleon. But this is sophistry, for under the Empire the victories of the *Patrie* are necessarily those of Napoleon. Again Vigny's thesis is affirmed: "Tout tourne mal dans les enseignements" (180–81) 'Teachings go completely awry.'

The third lesson alone, taught by experience, is morally determining. It occurs during the campaign of France in 1814. Renaud's company is ordered to scale some heights and take a Russian outpost. The men are to attack at night and with bayonets, so as not to give the alarm. They proceed to climb toward the enemy, disposing silently of sentries as they near their objective, a barn where the Russian soldiers are sleeping unawares. There follows what amounts to a massacre as Renaud's unit butchers the sleeping men: "Oh! ce fut une boucherie sourde et horrible! la baïonnette perçait, la crosse assommait, le genou étouffait, la main étranglait. Tous les cris à peine poussés étaient éteints sous les pieds de nos soldats, et nulle tête ne se soulevait sans recevoir le coup mortel" (198) 'What a silent, horrible slaughter it was! The bayonet pierced, the gun butt stunned, the knee stifled, the hand throttled. All their barely uttered cries were extinguished beneath our soldiers' feet, and not a head raised up without receiving a fatal blow.'

The carnage is done in a sinister silence broken only by stifled half cries. The scene is all the more grisly for its animation: the bayonet, the gun butt, the knee, the hand engage in both individual and collective acts of killing; separately depicted, their actions seem to multiply like those of disembodied automata from which the narrator stands curiously distinct. Yet, Renaud is implicated from the very first, for he has led the way into the barn and set the example by dealing the first blow, one that, to his horror, runs through a child, a young cadet officer about fourteen years old. Renaud is stunned. "—Etait-ce là un ennemi?" 'Was he an enemy?' he cries in anguish. Then he shows his colonel the body: "—Regardez cela, dis-je; quelle différence y a-t-il entre moi et un assassin?—Eh! sacrédié, mon cher, que voulez-vous? c'est le métier.—C'est juste, répondis-je" (200) '"Look at this," I said; "What difference is there between me and a murderer?" "Easy, man, what do you expect? It's our profession." "That's right," I replied.'

This "C'est juste" is ambiguous; it is not quite acceptance of the identity between war and murder, but it is certainly far from the old commandant's insistent "Oh! le métier, êtes-vous fou? ce n'est pas le métier!" 'Oh! The profession! Are you mad? It isn't the profession!' in "Laurette ou le cachet rouge." And in this very passage Renaud finds the child's malacca cane and decides henceforth to bear no other arms. This is his solution to the dilemma: to abandon his military career would be a denial; yet to continue to kill would constitute a violation of conscience. Renaud still marches upon the enemy (and when our author-narrator sees him in the July Days of 1830, that "enemy" is his fellow citizens!), but armed only with his *canne de jonc:* he is a soldier, for he may be killed, but he is a man because he refuses to kill.[14]

Yet, is this not really an evasion, a fiction? Renaud unarmed is no longer really a soldier, but a seeker after death. The spiritual

14. Here François Germain notes that "Renaud decides to sacrifice himself to his twin duties rather than sacrificing either of them" (lxix).

despondency pervading this scene extends from Renaud's obscure station to the highest rank, for when Renaud remarks to the surgeon that he is weary of war, a familiar voice echoes him with the words "Et moi aussi" 'And so am I.' The captain lifts his bandage to see "not Napoleon the emperor, but Bonaparte the soldier" (200). Thus even Napoleon, that is, Bonaparte, is humanized in this scene. His frailty and lassitude, that is, his humanity, are underscored when he deliberately advances upon a nearby fallen artillery shell, unexploded but still smoking. In this, his conduct is parallel to Renaud's marching unprotected toward death. It is not surprising that Renaud should feel himself reconciled to his master by this action; after the shell has exploded harmlessly, Renaud walks forward to shake Bonaparte's hand.

Here Renaud pauses, and we return to present time. Author-narrator Vigny reflects upon the progressively inward spectacle of the captain's soul: repulsed in its "expansive donations," its attempts at outward appurtenance or engagement, Renaud's soul has withdrawn to form an inner brilliance that suggests the formation of human conscience, a crystallization that implies permanence and peace.

Chaque vague de la mer ajoute un voile blanchâtre aux beautés d'une perle, chaque flot travaille lentement à la rendre plus parfaite, chaque flocon d'écume qui se balance sur elle lui laisse une teinte mystérieuse à demi dorée, à demi transparente, où l'on peut seulement deviner un rayon intérieur qui part de son coeur; c'était tout à fait ainsi que s'était formé ce caractère dans de vastes bouleversements et au fond des plus sombres et perpétuelles épreuves. (202)

With each wave the sea adds a milky veil to the beauties of a pearl, each billow slowly works to make it more perfect, each poised fleck of foam leaves a half-golden, half-transparent sheen, through which one can barely glimpse an inner beam radiating from its heart; it was in just this way that this man's character had been formed, amid vast turmoils and in the depths of somber and unending ordeals.

Georges Poulet wrote of this passage: "in Vigny, thanks to the contribution of the peripheral and the ephemeral, there is knowledge of the center, a perceptible development of the eternal."[15] Thus, the double notion of withdrawal and circularity leads to the distillation of conscience, which is truly eternal. Renaud, no longer a true fighting man, marches surrounded by soldiers. There are many such circular images in "La Canne de jonc": Renaud's alcove from which he witnesses the interview between Pius VII and Napoleon; the *réduit* that Renaud occupies on the *Victory;* a later ship, the *Ocean,* which is described as a "floating prison" (and having resisted the temptation to break his parole and escape, Renaud holds to its mainmast "as if to an asylum protecting me from dishonor"); Renaud's "hiding" in the army like "un chartreux dans son cloître" 'a monk in his cloister' and living there like the "prieur du couvent" 'monastery prior.'

All these constitute psychological spaces that are characteristically circumscribed, and all are vantage points that permit the elaboration of conscience. The circularity of Vigny's imagination prepares a "retour sur soi-même"[16] 'reabsorption' necessary to the absorption and condensation of experience. Even the enchased structure of the book, with its three tales within tales, this trinity enveloped within a narrative frame, may be related to these motifs. Turned upon itself, *Servitude et Grandeur militaires* has the very form of conscience.

Still, the ending of "La Canne de jonc" may appear to be excessively contrived. During the July Days, Renaud is shot in the thigh by a Parisian *gamin,* a young boy of "environ quatorze ans" (207) 'about fourteen years,' and dies of his wounds a few days later. Renaud thus expiates, rather talionically, his crime of

15. Georges Poulet, *Les Métamorphoses du cercle* (Paris, 1961), 235. Poulet also quoted with this passage, most appropriately, the lines beginning "Poésie, ô trésor, perle de la pensée!" (verse 134) 'Poetry, treasure and pearl of thought' from "La Maison du berger." A third passage may be mentioned in this context, namely the last stanza of "Les Oracles," which begins "Le DIAMANT, c'est l'art des choses idéales" 'The DIAMOND is the art of the ideal.' On the significance of the diamond for Vigny, see François Germain, *L'Imagination d'Alfred de Vigny* (Paris, 1962), 219 and Chapter 3, "L'Univers sphérique." The key image linking these passages is the *rayon,* the beam or beacon that bears witness to the molding of conscience and whose hard brilliance survives and illumines the ages. Such passages are thus related to Vigny's concept of experience's role in the formation of wisdom.

16. Vigny, *Journal,* II, 1050.

having killed the Russian child: he is in turn killed by his victim's reincarnation. At first glance this denouement is facile and inconsonant with the relatively sober and restrained tone of Vigny's narrative style. But the idea of the victim reincarnated as if to avenge himself on his assassin makes the scene pendant to the earlier scene of slaughter, and psychologically it is equivalent to that scene, as *gamin* and *enfant* are one and the same for Renaud. Moreoever, the ending provides the final resolution of two important motifs of "La Canne de jonc," those of the father and of silence.

There are many fathers, or at least paternal relationships, in "La Canne de jonc." First, there is Renaud's own father, briefly present at the start of the story to introduce the young Renaud to Bonaparte. But Renaud says that until the day of this introduction his father "m'était tout à fait inconnu" (140) 'was completely unknown to me,' and he is so immediately infatuated with Bonaparte that he feels that "il enlevait mon âme à mon père, que du reste je connaissais à peine parce qu'il vivait à l'armée éternellement" (143) 'he was stealing my soul away from my father, whom I scarcely knew, moreoever, since he was eternally away with the army.' Furthermore, the father departs without delay for the Egyptian campaign, leaving his son behind him, and is thereafter present only in the form of the letter sent during the period of captivity. He really counts only as an absence. He is the first of a pattern of fathers who are all absent fathers, foster (false) fathers, or dead fathers.[17] He is replaced by a foster father, Bonaparte, whose ambition Renaud is unwilling to accept and whom he flees.

Next Collingwood becomes a father to him, as well as teacher of the second lesson, which turns out badly. Collingwood is quite preoccupied about being so steadily absent from his two young daughters and says that he is only a letter (like Renaud's father) or a bit of advice to them: "On n'aime pas un conseil, on

---

17. These fatherly relationships are also discernible in "Laurette" and "La Veillée de Vincennes." Two fathers in "La Canne de jonc" that I leave undiscussed are the father of the *enfant russe* and the Holy Father, Pius VII (the spiritual father who offsets Bonaparte, the temporal father).

aime un être,—et un être qu'on ne voit pas n'est pas, on ne l'aime pas,—*et quand il est mort, il n'est pas plus absent qu'il n'était déjà*,—et on ne le pleure pas" (178; italics added) 'You don't love a piece of advice, you love a person—and a person you don't see doesn't exist and isn't loved—*and when he is dead, he's no more absent than he already was—and you don't weep for him*' (italics added).

I would suggest that this pattern of absent fathers is eschatological. It points to an absent Father, that is, a divine absence, a metaphysical emptiness that only the shaping of a moral and human conscience can fill. This moral independence (which is Vigny's concept of honor) is at last achieved in the end of "La Canne de jonc," where the negative pattern of absent fathers is broken (no priest attends Renaud's agony) and where Renaud becomes a genuinely spiritual father to Jean, the *gamin* who has shot him. Their bonds are bonds of conscience, for no happenstance of birth, religion, or rank dilutes the moral authenticity of their relationship. (Renaud has no children, and Jean is an "enfant trouvé" 'orphan.') They are not joined by abstract moral precepts; rather they share a common experience of death inflicted and received, and most important, they share honor. The dying Renaud stipulates that Jean shall never become a soldier, and through this promise Renaud himself, in extremis, renounces the military. Honor, a human virtue, is not to be found in those barren realms devoid of respect for the human: "L'honneur est le respect des hommes"[18] 'Honor is respect for mankind.' This is the universe of the "majesté des souffrances humaines" 'majesty of human sufferings' or the *strophe du silence* in Vigny's "Le Mont des oliviers."

> Muet, aveugle et sourd au cri des créatures,
> Si le Ciel nous laissa comme un monde avorté,
> Le juste opposera le dédain à l'absence
> Et ne répondra plus que par un froid silence
> Au silence éternel de la Divinité.
>
> Dumb, blind, and deaf to its creatures' cry,
> If Heaven has abandoned us like some aborted world,
> The just man will oppose scorn to absence

18. Vigny, *Journal*, II, 992. This sentence dates from 1833.

And reply with cold silence
To the eternal silence of the Divinity.

Here silence is joined to absence to suggest that the lessons of servitude must be learned in silence: the silence of the young *séide* hidden in the alcove and learning the truth about an ambitious Napoleon, the silence of the pope that signalizes the inviolability of his conscience, and the silence and solitude of Collingwood. And last and most important, Renaud expiates in silence the death of the *enfant russe:* "Je crains de parler . . . on s'affaiblit . . . je ne voudrais plus parler" (211) 'I'm afraid to speak . . . one turns weak . . . I no longer wish to speak.'

This is the silence of the wolf in "La Mort du loup." It is therefore in silence—in retreat, in renunciation—in the circumscription of the *tour d'ivoire* that conscience is forged. Renaud attains arduously to the permanence of conscience; he attains stasis in death. His final silence bears witness to the muteness of a vision that has in its anguish transcended the boundaries of verbal expression.

V 🐟 From Identity to Disarray in *La Chartreuse*

de Parme

I do not believe that anyone, even the late Henri Martineau, has ever established a definitive count of the names that Henri Beyle concocted for himself, but everyone knows that pseudonyms and *faux-fuyants* were his specialties. Louis-Alexandre-César Bombet, William Crocodile, Lisio Visconti, Dominique, and Baron de Cutendre are names that range from the waggish to the tender, from the public to the private. They reveal that to the Rabelais and the Falstaff in our author we must add a Cimarosa and an Ariosto,[1] to the Don Giovanni a Werther. The strutting boulevardier and raffish *salonnard* are doubled by the author of a treatise on love that vaunts, rather surprisingly, as the supreme happiness in sexual relations, "le premier serrement de main d'une femme qu'on aime"[2] 'the first squeeze of the hand of a woman we love.' As we shall soon see, Fabrice del Dongo experiences seraphic love in the Farnese Tower, a falling in love in which not even this pressure of the loved one's hand is felt—an "affair" transcending the terrestrial, a passion con-

---

1. See Robert M. Adams, *Stendhal: Notes on a Novelist* (New York, 1959), xiv.
2. Stendhal, *De l'Amour*, ed. Henri Martineau (Paris, 1959), 95. Compare with "Fragments divers," No. 32, in *De l'Amour*, 248.

sisting wholly of illusory delights, a new *amor che nella mente ragiona.*

Not to be divined, not to be found out was a constant preoccupation from the time of the four-year-old Henry Brulard's struggles in Grenoble with his Aunt Séraphie and the *noir coquin*, the abbé Raillane. "CACHE TA VIE" 'CONCEAL THY LIFE' the motto that best expresses this principle of conduct, will be shared by Octave de Malivert, Julien Sorel, Lucien Leuwen, and other Stendhalian heroes. Stendhal's many masks are usually taken to be evasions or sly concealments intended to disorient the *coeurs secs* and to thwart their pryings into an embarrassingly Romantic sensibility. The various uses of protective irony in the novels would constitute the stylistic equivalent of this protean mode, this desire for permanent metagenesis. Jean Starobinski, in a seminal essay,[3] quoted articles 3, 7, and 21 of *Les Privilèges du 10 avril 1840* in support of this view:

Vingt fois par an le privilégié pourra se changer en l'être qu'il voudra, pourvu que cet être existe. Cent fois par an, il saura pour vingt-quatre heures la langue qu'il voudra. . . . Le privilégié pourra, quatre fois par an, et pour un temps illimité chaque fois occuper deux corps à la fois.

Vingt fois par an, le privilégié pourra deviner la pensée de toutes les personnes qui sont autour de lui à vingt pas de distance. Cent vingt fois par an, il pourra voir ce que fait actuellement la personne qu'il voudra; il y a exception complète pour la femme qu'il aimera le mieux.[4]

Twenty times a year the beneficiary may be changed into the being of his desire, provided this being exists. One hundred times, he will know the language of his preference for twenty-four hours. . . . Four times a year, the beneficiary, for an unlimited time, may occupy two bodies at once.

Twenty times a year, the beneficiary may divine the thoughts of everyone within twenty feet of him. One hundred twenty times a year, he may see what anyone he wishes is doing at the moment; there is a complete exception for the woman he loves best.

The *Privilèges* are an extension and elaboration of an earlier passage in *Souvenirs d'égotisme.*

3. Jean Starobinski, "Stendhal pseudonyme," in Starobinski, *L'Œil vivant* (Paris, 1961), 191–244.
4. Stendhal, *Œuvres Intimes*, ed. Henri Martineau (Paris, 1966), 1525–30.

Me croira-t-on? Je porterais un masque avec plaisir, je changerais de nom avec délices. Les *Mille et Une Nuits* que j'adore occupent plus d'un quart de ma tête. Souvent je pense à l'anneau d'Angélique; mon souverain plaisir serait de me changer en un long Allemand blond, et de me promener ainsi dans Paris.[5]

Will anyone believe me? I would gladly wear a mask, would delight in changing my name. The *Thousand and one Nights*, which I adore, takes up more than a quarter of my mind. I often think of Angelica's ring; my sovereign pleasure would be to change into a slender blond German and thus to stroll through Paris.

Transmigration, ubiquity, metamorphosis: as Beyle becomes Stendhal, he finds that fiction alone offers these liberations. Who, after all, is Mina de Vanghel, if not that slender blonde German, enjoying Paris, she says, because she can go around incognito? Her sex is female, but she remains one of Stendhal's *Amazones*, those enterprisingly masculine heroines of whom we could say, as Julien does of Mathilde, "Le ciel devait à la gloire de ta race de te faire naître homme"[6] 'Heaven owed it to the glory of your ancestors to make you be born a man.'

But the mask in Stendhal is eventually much less an evasion or flight than it is an essay in personality and identity. First, the mask is a refusal to be typed. The most authentically Stendhalian characters follow an existentialist truism in that they learn about themselves in the heat of their actions. It is not knowledge that determines movement, but the reverse. In his comparison between Mathilde de la Mole and Mme de Rênal, Julien says: "Madame de Rênal trouvait des raisons pour faire ce que son coeur lui dictait: cette jeune fille du grand monde ne laisse son coeur s'émouvoir que lorsqu'elle s'est prouvé par bonnes raisons qu'il doit être ému" (I, 617–18) 'Madame de Rênal used to find reasons to do what her heart commanded; this society girl allows her heart to be moved only after she has shown with good arguments that it should be moved.' The theme of identity is linked then to the quest for self-knowledge, and the latter is

---

5. Stendhal, *Œuvres Intimes*, 1415–16.
6. Stendhal, *Romans et Nouvelles*, ed. Henri Martineau (Pléiade ed.; 2 vols.; Paris, 1964), I, 680. All page references to Stendhal's fiction in the text are to this edition.

particularly urgent to characters whose creator projects upon them his own feelings of estrangement. All of Stendhal's characters are presented as outsiders ("singulier" 'singular' is the prevalent adjective), and Stendhal is at great pains to underscore their uniqueness: Octave de Malivert and Lucien Leuwen are only children; Julien and Fabrice are near or real bastards.

A brief look at *Lucien Leuwen* shows that Lucien remains a shadowy character throughout the book, both to himself and to his creator. Lucien cannot settle on any particular station or place in life. Indeed, the unwritten third part of the novel was to have been called "Une Position sociale," the implication being that Lucien had yet to find such a position after several hundred pages of authorial labor. "Quel état prendre?" (I, 1199) 'What position shall I seek?' is Lucien's characteristic lament. Somewhat vexed, Stendhal asks himself in one of his final marginal notations, "Quel caractère a Lucien?" (I, 1575) 'What sort of character does Lucien have?' and remarks in unmistakable exasperation, "*The* plan a été ma *plague*" (I, 1588) 'The plot has been a plague to me.' The question of self-knowledge remains unresolved.

After abandoning *Lucien Leuwen*, Stendhal next undertook the writing of the autobiographical *Vie de Henry Brulard*, in which unfinished business is immediately brought to consideration. Noting that he is about to turn fifty, Stendhal reflects that it is "high time" he learned to know himself: "Qu'ai-je été, que suis-je, en vérité je serais bien embarrassé de le dire" 'What I've been, what I am, in truth I should be hard pressed to say.' Fiction and autobiography are never very far apart in Stendhal, and his novels are themselves trial identities, akin to essays—in the original sense of the word.

Speaking of etymologies, one of the first points to note about *La Chartreuse de Parme* is that the name Fabrizio suggests the Latin *fabrico* (to form, make, or forge); closer to our hero's world, it suggests the Italian *fabbro*. Fabrice does indeed turn out to be the *fabricator* (or artisan) of his soul. We may be tempted to find Fabrice del Dongo very different from his predecessors. Certainly no one would ever call Fabrice a "chien de *lisard*" (I, 234)

'damned bookworm,' as was the case with Julien. Reading, on
the other hand, always was a *vice impuni* in Stendhal's novels; it
is associated with the imitation of others and thus with inauthenticity.[7] Nor is Fabrice well educated; on the contrary, he is
described as "ignorant à plaisir et sachant à peine écrire" (II, 35)
'ignorant as can be, barely knowing how to write.' He learns to
read by deciphering the legends of engravings of Napoleonic
victories and learns what Latin he knows in the highly military
genealogy of the Valserra del Dongo family. This genealogy, incidentally, was devised by Fabrice's homonymic ancestor, the
archbishop of Parma, in 1650. It is more than piquant that later
in the novel Mosca should have the work translated into Italian
and attributed to Fabrice, for symbolically this makes Fabrice
the author of his own destiny, thus underscoring once again the
freedom of Stendhalian characters. If *Le Rouge et le Noir* and *La
Chartreuse de Parme* seem very different books to us, it is mainly
because of a difference in tone and attitude: Stendhal's bitter
irony in the chronicle of 1830 has dissolved into a mellow wry-
ness in the later book, but the characters and their ultimate vocation remain the same. Fabrice and Julien share an immoderate
love of military glory and an unwise admiration for Napoleon.[8]
Both seek their destiny in the flight of the eagle and the cry
of the osprey, though Clélia's domesticated birds stand for the
taming of this ambition. Both have their fates foretold in proleptic passages occurring on the saint's day of a martyred soldier—
Saint Clément in the case of Julien, San Giovita in the case of
Fabrice. Both have soaring imaginations, and imagination is a
morally purifying element in Stendhalian psychology.[9] Most
important, they eventually stand in contrast to the reactionary
Europe of the Congress of Vienna, the "triste dix-neuvième

---

7. F. W. J. Hemmings, *Stendhal: A Study of His Novels* (Oxford, 1964), 111–12. Jean-
Paul Weber, in his *Stendhal* (Paris, 1969), 476, noticed that Fabrice's name derives from
faber, but he linked it with the "thematic status of the worker."

8. Elsewhere Stendhal suggests that "a mad and necessarily unhappy ambition has
seized all the French" because Napoleon, an artillery lieutenant, was able to become
emperor and had raised several hundred citizens of similarly humble origins to the
heights of society. Stendhal, *Promenades dans Rome*, ed. Henri Martineau (Paris, 1931),
II, 182–83.

9. Hemmings, *Stendhal*, 120–21.

siècle" alluded to in the epigraph to one of the chapters of *Le Rouge et le Noir* (I, 612). The abbé Pirard says to Julien, "je vois en toi quelque chose qui offense le vulgaire" (I, 403), 'I see something in you that offends common men,' and Gina tells Fabrice, "Vous déplairez toujours aux hommes, vous avez trop de feu pour les âmes prosaïques" (II, 51) 'You will always displease men, you have too much fire for prosaic souls.'[10]

Fabrice's disguises, on the level of plot, enable him to escape the requirements, even the persecutions, of a hostile society, but they are essentially related to self-knowledge and the continued possibility for change. Old age is not a question of gray hair or calendar years. In Stendhal the old are not necessarily shriveled by the years; rather they are shriveled by their inability to change.[11]

Fabrice's first disguise is a military costume. His aunt encourages him in this fancy. Through her influence in the court of Prince Eugène, her twelve-year-old nephew is breveted *officier de hussards*, and she is enchanted by the figure he cuts in his little uniform. Several years later, his head filled with tales of Napoleonic glory, Fabrice not unexpectedly rushes to join the emperor after his return from Elba. He avoids the vigilance of the Austrian police by using the identity of his friend Vasi, the barometer salesman. From this point onward, Fabrice's identities never cease to multiply. Jailed as a suspected spy, he is able to escape with the papers of the *hussard* who died in prison, a terrible coincidence and presage to his superstitious mind: "Gare la prison! . . . Le présage est clair, j'aurai beaucoup à souffrir de la prison!" (II, 55) 'Beware of prison! . . . The omen is clear, I shall have much to suffer from prisons!' Upon the battlefield of Waterloo the motherly *vivandière* takes him for a misguided, lovestruck youth. Later, in the heat of the fight, Fabrice is asked his identity and passes himself off as the brother-in-law of a Captain Meunier or Teulier. Soon he imagines that

---

10. In *Le Rouge et le Noir* there are numerous references to Julien's *feu sacré*. Compare, particularly, *De l'Amour*, Chapter 22, "De l'engouement."

11. See Victor Brombert's chapter on *La Chartreuse de Parme* (subtitled "The Poetry of Freedom") in his *Stendhal: Fiction and the Themes of Freedom* (New York, 1968), 149–76.

between himself and the officers with whom he is galloping there exists the noble friendship of Tasso and Ariosto's heroes. Even after our "heroic parasite" has been unhorsed by his own father and wounded in his barring of the bridge of the *auberge du Cheval Blanc*, he cannot hide his essential strangeness.[12] The *vivandière*—after asking, "Who are you, *really?*"—advises him to take on a disguise to escape the military police, and while he is recovering from his wounds in a little Flemish village, the mistress of the inn and her daughters take him for a "prince in disguise" (II, 91).

Stendhal's heroes are certainly outsiders, but they are not the stock outcasts of European Romanticism, such as the figure of the artist in Byron or Vigny, or the outlaw in Hugo or Balzac. Fabrice stands out because his roles never seem to suit him and because his masks are constantly slipping. One must wear a mask, for simplicity is suspect in an age of cant.[13] F. W. J. Hemmings notes that one of the most widely held assumptions about Stendhal's heroes is that they strive to live up to their image and that Fabrice is the exception: "Having accepted that self-examination is sinful, [Fabrice] never asks where he is going, he never wonders what sort of man he is. . . . In psychological parlance, Fabrice is 'integrated.' His life is as unorientated as Lucien's but, unlike Lucien, he is completely untroubled by the fact."[14]

The intent and result of Stendhal's mock-epic treatment of Waterloo is to purge Fabrice of his dreams of military glory. Fabrice crosses the Italian border with another false identity, that of a certain Cavi, occupation unknown, and finally makes his way to the paternal manor disguised first as a hunter and then as a smuggler. As his aunt and mother are rushing him off to Milan, he is mistakenly arrested in the place of General Fabio Conti, which is certainly one of the novel's greatest comic ironies. Moreoever, this whole scene abounds in mistaken identities and unconscious revelations of destiny. It will be remembered

12. Brombert, *Stendhal*, 155.
13. Stendhal, *Correspondance*, ed. Henri Martineau (10 vols.; Paris, 1934), VI, 114.
14. Hemmings, *Stendhal*, 184.

that here Fabrice sees Clélia for the first time. She is surrounded by *gendarmes*, and at the sight of her Fabrice exclaims to himself, "Ce serait une charmante compagne de prison" (II, 99) 'She would be a charming prison companion.' The linked identity-destiny theme is particularly well handled in this scene, with its complex blending of irony, comedy, and poetic prediction. At last Fabrice is able to extricate himself by passing for his brother Ascagne, and he then proceeds toward Romagnan, there to expiate his Napoleonic escapade by feigning great piety—attending mass every day—and great passion for a mistress to be chosen in an ultra family. In the eyes of society (and of Metternich's police), this line of conduct will establish him as an innocuous nobleman with no untoward interest in politics. But, Stendhal notes, "il n'y avait pas encore de place pour *l'imitation des autres* dans cette âme naïve et ferme, et il ne fit pas d'amis dans la société du gros bourg de Romagnan; sa simplicité passait pour de la hauteur; on ne savait que dire de ce caractère" (II, 109) 'there was as yet no room for the *imitation of others* in that innocent and sturdy soul, and he made no friends in the large town of Romagnan; his simplicity passed for arrogance; people didn't know what to make of his character.'

Subsequently Fabrice will disguise himself as a domestic of the casa del Dongo, as Giletti (the actor he is accused of murdering), as a theology student, as the valet of an English lord, as a duelist, as a chestnut vendor, and, on two occasions, even as a priest—a delightful disguise for monsignor del Dongo! One of these occasions is Fabrice's escape from the Farnese tower: Clélia urges him to cast off his prisoner's clothing and to don priest's garb the better to make his escape. The implication is that Clélia—quite rightly—views Fabrice's priest identity as a disguise. Much earlier a passage with a similar implication described Fabrice's easygoing manner in the archbishop's palace, stressing his difficulty in putting on the airs of a *grand seigneur*. The point is that Fabrice *is* a great lord by birth and should have no trouble being one. But again, this is manifestly an identity that does not "stick"; like so many other masks, it does not represent his true self. Here we may think of the young bishop of

Agde in *Le Rouge et le Noir:* Fabrice has become just such a
bishop (or at least a *grand vicaire*), but he never thinks of rehearsing his role in front of a full-length mirror.

Let us also consider one of the most puzzling scenes in *La
Chartreuse,* one that is rarely, if ever, mentioned in criticism.
I refer to the scene in which the jealous protector of La Fausta,
who has mistaken Fabrice for the Prince of Parma, has him
seized one night by a band of *bravi,* thrust into a sedan chair,
and paraded around Parma in a bizarre procession led by a hundred torches, with all the participants professing a sinister def-
erence for "His Highness." This mock ceremony is a parody
of the papal *sedia gestatoria* and an ironic accomplishment of
Blancs' prediction that Fabrice would die one day sitting on a
wooden seat. The intertextual reference, we know today, is to
Alessandro Farnese, the dissolute protagonist of the Italian
chronicle that was the source of *La Chartreuse,* "Origine delle
grandezze della famiglia Farnese." This member of the powerful Italian family eventually became pope under the name of
Paul III. Fabrice is hardly *papabile,* so the sense of the episode
would appear to involve another purging of Stendhal's charac
ter. That is, Stendhal ironically purges Fabrice of whatever vestige of ecclesiastical identity may have remained in his destiny.
Once again he has forestalled his character's choice of either the
red or the black.

Fabrice's destiny and identity are both simpler and more complex. "Tout est simple à ses yeux parce que tout est vu de haut"
(II, 156) 'In his eyes everything is simple, because everything is
seen from above,' says Mosca of Fabrice, and this phrase rather
neatly expresses the moral sense of Stendhal's prison metaphor.
De l'Amour tells us that the great man is like an eagle: the more
he is raised, the less visible he is, but he is punished for his
greatness by the loneliness of his soul.[15] Earlier I mentioned
Fabrice's nonreflective approach to life. But there is of course
one question that constantly worries him, and that is why he
seems to lack a capacity for love. It is strange, he thinks, that he

15. Stendhal, *De l'Amour,* 50.

is not susceptible to that "passionate and exclusive preoccupation" (II, 224) called love. He is thus more convinced than ever that his destiny will forever deny him knowledge of the "noble and intellectual part of love" (II, 244).

So ends Part I of *La Chartreuse de Parme*. With his imprisonment Fabrice is soon thoroughly convinced that before seeing Clélia he had never been in love and that "la destinée de sa vie était de ne vivre que pour elle" (II, 350) 'the destiny of his life was to live only for her.' Before his imprisonment (which leads to self-discovery), Fabrice del Dongo's multiple identities may be looked upon as symbolic trials; after his escape they are protective disguises of the self. Love is the vocation of Stendhal's characters. But we must add that the world of love is never perfectly attained; it remains an unfulfilled promise. The myth of perfect love is impossible here, for love in Stendhal is not a state but an eternal becoming. Stendhal's characters retain their independence and are spared the disappointments of aging. Love flees their grasp and represents Stendhal's *chasse au bonheur*.

The blissful sojourn in the Farnese Tower has been well described: its intensified, protected vision of the loved one, the musical purity of the communication between the lovers. Its aerial and moral elevation are raptures that Stendhal situates outside and above the pettiness and strife of ordinary existence.

Clélia's orange trees, with their fragile and artificial existence, mediate the passage from the harsh realities of political Parma to the illusory realm of the Farnese Tower. Orange blossoms are traditionally symbols of virginity and marriage, and here they stand for the flowering of love. Earlier in the novel Clélia had meditated upon "that terrible passion, love" near some orange trees of the palace, and now, on the very evening that Fabrice is imprisoned, she has similar trees brought up to her aerial domain. (The passage contains striking analogies with one in *Ernestine* in which the eponymous heroine also takes refuge in a Stendhalian "high place," where she cares for caged birds, gazes at the view from behind the protection of slatted windows to think unrestrainedly of her loved one, and tends bouquets of flowers.) The ephemeral, precarious life of these orange trees figures the tenuous nature of the love illusion into which Fabrice and Clélia move.

It is also worth examining the circumstances of Fabrice's departure from this earthly paradise. His escape is a return to reality, and its stages permit us to catalogue, *a contrario* as it were, the extent of illusions lost in his descent.

The episode is first of all marked by an apparent loss of narrative control, something highly unusual in the case of an author reluctant ever to relinquish his post as master of ceremonies. What I mean by this is that his customary briskness of narrative style—rich and varied in intrusions, parenthetical remarks, and asides of all kinds—appears to falter in the escape scene, and the heretofore all-controlling narrator yields to unnamed witnesses for his narrative information. They now become the reader's sources, as if Stendhal had suddenly remembered his embedded, second-degree narrator, the nephew of a Padua canon briefly mentioned in the preface and soon forgotten, who kept him up all night with the story of the Duchesse de Sanseverina. Thus, at the moment Fabrice, dangling from his first rope, passes before the eyes of two hundred soldiers comically transformed into a row of windows "bristling with bayonets," he is seized by a moment of "folly": "Some people have claimed that Fabrice, mad as usual, had the notion of playing the devil's role, and that he threw a fistful of sequins to these soldiers."[16] Just who are these "people"? Their appearance marks a narrative distancing without precedent in *La Chartreuse*, and when the narrator adds that what *is* certain is that Fabrice spread sequins over the floor of his room, he abandons authorial certainty and seems now to disavow his own responsibility: "Ce qui paraît incroyable et pourrait faire douter du fait si le résultat n'avait eu pour témoins une ville entière" 'Which seems incredible and could make one doubt the fact if the whole town had not been witness to the fact.'

16. On "folie," see Shoshana Felman, *La "Folie" dans l'oeuvre romanesque de Stendhal* (Paris, 1974).

Moreover, certain narrative tenses impose a perspective that is far from Jean Pouillon's being "with" the character or Gérard Genette's "internal focalization" and becomes that of an *ex post facto* telling that again sets the reader at a remove from the event.[17] Thus, "Fabrice said that when he was on the platform . . ." "He added that . . ." "'I wasn't bothered in the least,' he added. 'It seemed to me as though I were carrying out a ceremony.'" All the details of the escape fade into the haziness of a dream. In the midst of his descent Fabrice *thinks* that he let go of the cord for an instant, and *perhaps* he took hold of bushes growing in the walls. His defective perception causes him to fall on a *small* acacia tree that in reality is fifteen or twenty feet tall. Pulling himself together, Fabrice takes a drink of brandy and even lies down to nap for a few moments "to the point of not knowing where he was. . . . At last the frightening truth came back to him." His flight ends with a second fall, for his third rope is a bit short (he unrolls scarcely fewer ropes than he had mounted horses at Waterloo!) and he falls into a trench of muddy water. Then he lapses into a "deep" faint.

The reader is thus faced with an unusual double phenomenon: on one hand Stendhal appears to "release" his narrative, as it were, and on the other to break and even invert the ascensional thrust that had so forcefully marked the two prison novels. Victor Brombert has linked the admixture of the precise and the vague in this scene to the process of Fabrice's rebirth.[18] What is Stendhal up to? The components of the escape episode warrant careful examination.

Fabrice's perilous adventure is not a novel undertaking in the Stendhalian canon. His treatment of this episode is very close to the mock-epic treatment of Waterloo, if indeed it is not its exact counterpart. The battle of Waterloo—the loudest "pistol shot" of Stendhal's oeuvre to the extent that it inaugurates the "sad nineteenth century"—is greeted by Fabrice with

17. Gérard Genette, "Discours du récit," in Genette, *Figures III* (Paris, 1972).
18. See Victor Brombert, "Les Douceurs de la prison," in Brombert, *La Prison romantique: Essai sur l'imaginaire* (Paris, 1975), 67–92.

a boundless happiness, and the day of his flight he awakens feeling "allègre et dispos" 'alert and fit.' In both episodes our hero acts heroically, or at least bravely exposes himself to danger (which amounts to the same in Fabrice's case), and finds himself projected into chivalric times, with evocations at Waterloo of Tasso and Ariosto. He has pious thoughts of Clélia at the moment of his departure, "like a hero of the age of chivalry." Most of all, each exploit marks the end of an illusion: Waterloo, that of war and the escape, that of love. These episodes constitute rites of passage, and both are experienced as ceremonials of disenchantment. Fabrice is right to feel that he is accomplishing "une cérémonie." At Waterloo each rise into the saddle was followed by an unseating; the descent from the citadel is uninterrupted but irreversible. At Waterloo, Fabrice "défaisait un à un tous ses beaux rêves d'amitié chevaleresque et sublime" 'abandoned one by one all his fine dreams of chivalric and sublime friendship'; leaving the "aerial solitude" of the Farnese Tower, he sees his dreams change into a nightmarish world. Not only had Fabrice discovered that his heart could love, but he seemed to have realized Julien's dream—the Julien who lamented that the only bad thing about prison was the impossibility of locking the door from the inside—for Fabrice's cell was equipped with an inner bolt. The "real" world constantly solicits us: "Le feu a pris au château" 'The castle has taken fire.' Is the escape signal a reference to the castle-prison from which Fabrice will be twice expelled? And when he answers, "Mes livres sont-ils brûlés?" 'Are my books burned?' the question concerns the permanence of his love, for his only books in prison were those fashioned from the alphabets torn out of breviaries, the means by which the lovers' discourse was reinvented. Fabrice must abandon a sun-filled world for a gloomy one; henceforth existence will be perceived only through absence or negation. The components of his former happiness will be conveyed *à rebours*, by a series of reversed images.

To begin with, there is the bundle of ropes that Fabrice uncoils as he makes his escape. Far from being the tenuous threads of an

Ariadne, woven by love, the thick cords move him away from love. There are three of them (35, 180, and 23 feet in length), and they encumber his descent.

Il avait fait quelques noeuds seulement à l'immense corde nécessaire pour descendre de cette terrible hauteur de cent quatre-vingts pieds. Il arrangea cette corde en bandoulière autour de son corps: elle le gênait beaucoup, son volume était énorme; les noeuds l'empêchaient de former masse, et elle s'écartait à plus de dix-huit pouces du corps. (II, 379)

He had made some fresh knots only in the immense cord necessary to come down from that terrible height of 180 feet. He draped the cord like a bandolier around his body: it greatly encumbered him because of its enormous volume; the knots prevented it from being wound close, and it protruded more than 18 inches from his body.

Moreover, the sign to leave is the equivalent of an imposed darkness: Clélia will be dressed in black and a little after midnight will leave only a small lamp next to the birdcage. This damping of love, which looks forward to the clandestine night meetings in the Crescenzi palace, moves Fabrice to action. His first gesture also is to deprive himself of all light, for he is obliged to turn his back to Clélia in order to climb down the "mur du couchant" 'the wall facing the sunset,' designated by Ferrante Palla as the most favorable to his escape. Night falls, and Fabrice puts on priest's garb to slip through the thick fog that envelops the citadel.

This fog, propitious to his flight, is the enemy of the love idyll. Fabrice had indeed shown little enthusiasm for the idea of escape, fearing "un exil affreux où tout manquera, jusqu'à l'air pour respirer" (II, 355) 'an atrocious exile in which everything would be lacking, even air to breathe.' The fog is thus opposed to the clarity of the love vision and the pureness of its sensations. One has only to think of the "sublime spectacle" offered by the Emilian panorama on the first day of his incarceration: then the moon and the sun conspired to illuminate before his delighted eyes the tops of the immense wall of the Alps. From their snowfields emanated "une sorte de fraîcheur par souvenir au milieu de ces campagnes brûlantes; l'oeil peut en suivre les moindres détails" (II, 308) 'a sort of remembered coolness in the midst of the scorching plains; the eye can follow their slightest details.' Stendhal's taste for Mozart's sharp, distinct notes is well known, and the reader, by contrast, measures the loggy feeling and atmosphere of unconsciousness that accompany the fog. ("He acted mechanically, he said.")

The crystalline silence of amorous isolation is now succeeded by discordant and vulgar noises. There are Fabrice's own steps, as he tiptoes across the curved tiles of the guardroom roof, and the joking laughter of two hundred soldiers drunk on quadruple rations of wine and barrels of brandy given by an "unknown hand" (again, Clélia's handiwork). This rotgut liquor itself (and one thinks of the poisons Gina has provided Fabrice) is opposed in context to the heady prison bubbly, the sparkling *nébieu d'Asti* of the love cell. And in the course of his escape, Fabrice nearly awakens a drunkard—hardly an Edenic personage—at the foot of the great wall.

This rupturing of silence warrants a few additional remarks. At the time of the idyll, the calm had been punctuated only by communicative circuits that augmented its serene character, for example, Clélia's recitative warning Fabrice of Barbone's attempt to poison him (on the perhaps specious level of phonetics, the threatening "Barbone" succeeds the laughing "Grillo") and the chirping from Clélia's birdcage—"captive" images that figure the taming of the hero's wild passions, formerly inflamed by the majestic flight of the Napoleonic eagle (during the descent Fabrice will be attacked by "rather large" birds). Fabrice is sensitive only to the *form* of this message and to the fact of the communication itself; he pretends not to understand its content. The episode allows Stendhal to renew a worn conceit of Renaissance love language, "the music of her words," and allows Fabrice to establish, through the alphabets, the contact he had been seeking with "three months of effort." It is important to note that these conversations, carried out by means of letters drawn on pages torn out of a breviary, amount not only to a reinvention, from *A* to *Z*, of the language of love—the "sacred

language" that Stendhal had spoken of in *Promenades dans Rome*—
but also to a harmonizing of profane and sacred love.[19] Moreover, the communicative channel expands at the will of its privileged users. During its first test—a critical moment of life or
death for Fabrice—it absorbs the transmission of no fewer than
sixty-five words. To the usual flow of discursivity, it opposes a
qualitative intensification that could be termed negentropic.
This is the explanation for the famous question, "Que serait la
conversation de salon, comparée à celle qu'ils faisaient avec des
alphabets?" (II, 344) 'How could a drawing-room conversation
compare with the one they carried on with the alphabets?'

After the musical intercession, the lovers, in the aerial purity
of the silence, make use of this graphic procedure, which
amounts to a re-creation of the Word. Immersed in that silence,
words swell and grow into being and substance. Like the Japanese game of the little pieces of paper Proust describes in "Combray," their words "s'étirent, se contournent, se colorent, se dif-
férencient" 'stretch, twist, take on color and shape.' Filling a
void and creating a space of their own, they make the passage
from a state of disorder (the Greek chaos or the *tohubohu* of
Genesis) to that of an organized shape. The affirmation that at
the end of his nine months in prison Fabrice was another man is
to be taken *au pied de la lettre*, literally: "Combien je suis différ-
ent, se dit-il, du Fabrice léger et libertin qui entra ici il y a neuf
mois!" 'How different I am, he said, from the fickle and liber-
tine Fabrice who entered here nine months ago!' The return to
the realm of the spoken, the sayable, is a distressing fall. At the
end of his escape, Fabrice no longer has the strength (or perhaps
the will) to "speak or open his eyes." He is awakened by another
sense, smell, the one that is linked most surely with the depths
of distant memory: "Ce parfum le ranima; il ouvrit les yeux; il
put prononcer les mots: Ah! chère amie! Puis il s'évanouit de
nouveau profondément" 'The scent of the duchess' clothing re-
vived him; he opened his eyes and could barely speak these
words: Ah, dear friend! Then he fell again into a deep faint.'

19. See J. D. Hubert's classic article, "Notes sur la dévaluation du réel dans *La
Chartreuse de Parme*," *Stendhal Club*, V (October 15, 1959), 47–53.

The broken style or syntactic discontinuities that mark the end of the passage gesture toward the relearning of a disremembered, inferior language.

The negative conversion of the paradisiacal is emphasized, too, by Fabrice's designation as the "devil on the roof" by the drunken soldiers who hear his steps overhead. And Fabrice plays the role of tempter, throwing them a handful of sequins and strewing the floor of his cell with more sequins. Driven by a "supernatural force," Fabrice now is resolved cold-bloodedly to stab the first guard who makes a move toward him. He will no longer be the "devil's dupe," as he had been upon his return from Grianta in the imprudent affair of the horse "purchased" for twenty francs—but stolen just the same. Now that he knows what the real stake in his life is, Fabrice is able to put into practice one of Mosca's vigorous maxims: "Il vaut mieux tuer le diable que si le diable vous tue" (II, 184) 'It's better to kill the devil than let the devil kill you.' But the price for such wisdom is the abandonment, even if it is an unwilling one, of the cellular paradise. The fatal aspect of his flight is measured by his very descent, which is contrary to all the injunctions of Abbé Blanès: "Prends garde de tomber, ce serait d'un affreux présage" (II, 178) 'Take care not to fall; that would be an awful omen.' It is certainly ominous that Fabrice should have two falls during his escape and that one of these is on the top of the acacia, a movement that is the contrary of the vertical thrust of his chestnut tree, his tree of Jesse, of "monachal ascension," according to Gilbert Durand.[20] To the fall in space corresponds a fall into temporality—"about one in the morning," "about midnight," "about half past midnight"—and this acute sense of the passing of time is opposed to the feeling of eternity he had experienced in prison.

Stendhal underscores these discordances by making a different narrative voice heard in this episode. Whereas formerly the reader was close to events, through contemporaneous narration, here he is distanced by the retrospective narrative stance. Thus,

20. Gilbert Durand, *Le Décor mythique de "la Chartreuse de Parme"* (Paris, 1961), 53.

the reader, with Fabrice, feels disorientation, confusion, as if of a world inverted.

In love Fabrice has found his identity; he has also found self-knowledge. Stendhal stands in the long tradition of French *moralistes* who believe, from La Rochefoucauld to Proust, that love provides the most revealing vantage point for the science of the heart. Without *amour-passion* there would be no self-knowledge; indeed, as Margaret Tillett has written, there would be "no self at all, only a *peut-être*."[21]

21. Margaret Tillett, *Stendhal: The Background to the Novels* (London, 1971), 78.

VI The Madame Bovary Blues

The time has long passed since readers saw in *Madame Bovary*, above all, the deflation of Romantic myth and in its narrative strategies what Baudelaire called Flaubert's "systematic harshness" toward the characters and what the Goncourts—more biographically—referred to as his "heartlessness." Readers have come to realize that *bovarysme* is nothing less than the tragedy of dreams—as Victor Brombert once phrased it, the "tragedy of the very absence of Tragedy."[1] *Madame Bovary* stands for a great deal more than the historical chart of a lost and compromised principality in the realm of human sensibility. For it is clear that while we are certainly witnessing the deflation of a myth in this novel—what Flaubert himself designated as the illusory existence of "contrées dithyrambiques" 'dithyrambic lands'—that deflation in no sense invalidates the myth's urgency or even destroys it.[2] Nearly all critics have been sensitive to the novel's not-so-hidden message, which might be put as Harry Levin indeed put it—that "*Madame Bovary c'est nous*," that is,

1. Victor Brombert, *The Novels of Flaubert* (Princeton, 1966), 90.
2. Gustave Flaubert, *Madame Bovary*, ed. Claudine Gothot-Mersch (Paris, 1971), 40. All page references in the text are to this edition.

that *Madame Bovary* simultaneously enshrines and profanes pretensions common to all men and women.[3]

How is this feat of preservation and destruction accomplished? How does Flaubert manage to retrieve as much as he ultimately discredits? What are the "original ways" of Flaubert? To these questions the careful reflections of generations of Flaubert scholars have yielded an array of responses. The most familiar are perhaps the studies of Flaubert's masterful deployment of *style indirect libre*, his use of ironic juxtapositions and his patterning of recurring images, particularly in the novel's insistent, multiple circularities. Hosts of critics have applied their intelligence and ingenuity to the scrutiny of the novelist's art, to the understanding of the craft of a work provocatively called by its author "ce livre tout en calcul et en ruses de style."[4]

In the 1970s, critical emphasis shifted from narratorial stance toward the phenomenon of writing itself, largely in the wake of Roland Barthes' analysis of textual resistance, what he was to erect into the oppositional relationship of the *lisible* to the *scriptible*. For Barthes, the classical mode of transparent narrativity was to yield in the course of nineteenth-century French fiction to an opaque *textuality:* a thickening and foregrounding of scriptural play—the play of free-floating signifiers—that superseded classical closure. He himself thus inaugurated a type of erasure going beyond what Flaubert often demanded of the author, namely self-effacement in the name of objectivity. Proust admired the phenomenality of Flaubert's descriptions: "Dans [ses] grandes phrases les choses existent non pas comme l'accessoire d'une histoire, mais dans la réalité de leur apparition" 'In [his] grand phrases things exist not as the accessories of the story, but in the reality of their apparition.'[5] But Barthes saw rather an ironic disavowal.

L'écriture classique . . . s'essouffle vite, se ferme et signe très tôt son dernier code. . . . Flaubert cependant . . . en maniant une ironie frappée

3. Harry Levin, *The Gates of Horn* (New York 1963), 263.
4. Gustave Flaubert, *Correspondance*, ed. Jean Bruneau (Paris, 1980), May 21, 1853.
5. Marcel Proust, "A ajouter à Flaubert," in Proust, *Contre Sainte-Beuve*, ed. Pierre Clarac (Paris, 1971), 299.

d'incertitude, opère un malaise (ou l'arrête mal), en sorte que (c'est là sans doute la preuve de l'écriture) *on ne sait jamais s'il est responsable de ce qu'il écrit* (s'il y a un sujet *derrière* son langage); car l'être de son écriture (le sens du travail qui la constitue) est d'empêcher de jamais répondre à cette question: *Qui parle?* (italics in original)

Classical writing quickly runs out of breath, closes and very soon signs its last code. . . . Flaubert, however . . . by maintaining an irony marked by uncertainty, creates a malaise (or does little to avoid it), so that (here no doubt is the test of writing) *one never knows if he is responsible for what he writes* (if there is a subject *behind* his language); for the essence of his writing (the sense of the labor that constitutes it) is to prevent this question from ever being answered: *who is speaking?* (italics in original)[6]

In a similar vein Jonathan Culler argues against criticism's insistence on *recuperation:* "the desire to leave no chaff, to make everything wheat, to let nothing escape but integrate it in a larger scheme by giving it meaning. . . . We admit to and tolerate an absence of meaning in nature but we are ill-prepared to do so in culture."[7] Indeed, the temptation to view every shred of novelistic detail as motivated has spawned close—microscopically close—readings in which not the slightest possibility of "natural" elements is entertained, in which a cigar could scarcely ever be "just a cigar."[8]

However, attempts to identify moments of purely scriptural activity in the Flaubertian text have been problematic at best. Again, we may turn to another influential concept of Barthes', the *effet de réel—the reality effect.* In the article introducing the concept, Barthes asserted that the description of Rouen in Part III of *Madame Bovary* acquired meaning not through its conformity to documentary accuracy but through its conformity to the cultural rules governing representation.[9] Unfortunately for the fate of both the reality effect and the unrecuperable, Mieke Bal has convincingly shown that there exists a high degree of

---

6. Roland Barthes, *S/Z* (Paris, 1971), 146.

7. Jonathan Culler, *Flaubert: The Uses of Uncertainty* (Ithaca, N.Y., 1974), 22.

8. See Tony Tanner's chapter on *Madame Bovary* in his *Adultery and the Novel* (Baltimore, 1979).

9. Roland Barthes, "L'Effet de réel," *Communications*, XI (1968), 84–89. This article was translated as "The Reality Effect" in Tzvetan Todorov (ed.), *French Literary Theory Today* (Cambridge, England, 1982), 7–11.

indexation, that is, of thematic coding, between this allegedly "empty" text and the diegetic web that interconnects the entire novel.[10] In sum, the rather ancient rapprochement of text and *textile*, the image of weaving as metaphor of story-making, seems after all not to have been fabricated out of whole cloth. Thus, in the central weave of Flaubert's text are recurring images (leitmotifs, semiotic coding), guiding and conditioning reader response to Emma's particular universe. Many such filiations have been traced over the years, for example the spider webs, the plaster priest, and the three Cupids.[11] The effect of these encodings is often difficult to gauge, but I should like to attempt a limited assessment by tracking the polysemous appearances of a single lexical element—blue (and its allomorphs). For this color is perhaps more intimately linked to the sentimental core of *Madame Bovary* than any other single word.

Blue is mentioned more than fifty times in the course of the novel. Some of its uses may indeed designate purely exterior referents such as the sky or peasant blouses. But more interesting is the process of encoding that attaches to *azur* and especially *bleuâtre*, words that evoke Emma's intertwined mystical and sensual longings. The famous flashback relating Emma's convent education—"Elle avait lu *Paul et Virginie* et elle avait rêvé la maisonnette de bambous" (36) 'She had read *Paul et Virginie* and dreamt of the bamboo hut'—introduces us for the first time to the languor and voluptuousness, the "warm atmo-

10. See the chapter entitled "Descriptions (pour une théorie de la description narrative); à propos de *Madame Bovary* de Flaubert" in Bal's *Narratologie* (Paris, 1977), 87–111. More recently, Dennis Porter has argued for a *chosisme* in Flaubert from *Salammbô* on: "Flaubert and the Difficulty of Reading," *Nineteenth-Century French Studies*, XII (1983), 366–78. He has also identified a "texte de plaisir" (another Barthes term) in *Madame Bovary:* "*Madame Bovary* and the Question of Pleasure," in Naomi Schor and Henry F. Majewski (eds.), *Flaubert and Postmodernism* (Lincoln, 1984), 116–38. Graham Falconer, following Barthes, also proposes an "empty" passage: "Reading *L'Education sentimentale:* Belief and Disbelief," *Nineteenth-Century French Studies*, XII (1983), 329–43. A judiciously balanced view of the matter is presented in P. M. Wetherill, "Flaubert et les incertitudes du texte," in Wetherill, *Flaubert: La dimension du texte* (Manchester, England, 1982), 255–70.

11. See, respectively, Richard B. Grant, "The Role of Minerva in *Madame Bovary*," *Romance Notes*, VI, (1965), 133–45; Brombert, *The Novels of Flaubert*, 48–49; and Alfred G. Engstrom, "Flaubert's Correspondence and the Ironic and Symbolic Structure of *Madame Bovary*," *Studies in Philology*, XLVI (1949), 470–95.

sphere," that inform Emma's reveries: "Elle s'assoupit doucement à la langueur mystique qui s'exhale des parfums de l'au-
tel. . . . Au lieu de suivre la messe, elle regardait dans son livre
les vignettes pieuses bordées d'*azur*" (37) 'She was sweetly lulled
by the mystical languor exhaled from the altar perfumes. . . .
Instead of following the mass, she looked in her book at the
pious vignettes edged in *azure*.'[12] Emma reads Scott and dream-
ily projects herself into the dreamlands that she finds in her
friends' keepsakes. Nor is it frivolous to mention that incense
has a characteristically bluish haze, for in Part II, when Emma
remembers and longs to return to her convent existence, she
seems to see the sweet face of the Virgin amid the "bluish swirls
of the incense" (113). The link between Emma's religiosity and
her sensuality is too well known to require justification here—
Flaubert more than once explicity indicates that there is no distinction between profane and sacred love for Emma—but the
stylistic link between the varieties of seraphic spheres that Emma
seeks is blue. The bluish swirls just mentioned cannot help but
be associated with Emma's brief sojourn at La Vaubyessard during which her soul seems at last to merge with her ideal; her
personality dissolves itself into the vicomte's world, as Flaubert
wrote in a discarded simile, like "une goutte de vin rouge que
l'on laisse tomber dans un verre d'eau" 'a drop of red wine falling into a glass of water.'[13] As Emma turns and turns in the
arms of the vicomte, a truly Baudelairean *valse mélancolique et
langoureux vertige*, their heady waltz becomes the bodily equivalent of those bluish swirls in a world composed of the blue
sheen of Emma's bandeaux, of cavaliers "dressed in blue," of
"myosotis" and "bleuets" (51–53).

These mentions of blue might seem arbitrary and unconvinc-
ing were it not for two key usages of *bleuâtre*, each dominating a
passage evoking Emma's imaginative transfigurations of her
"destined" existence with, respectively, Rodolphe and Léon. It

12. Here and throughout the remainder of the chapter, all italics within quotations
from the novel have been added except where noted otherwise.
13. Gustave Flaubert, *Madame Bovary, nouvelle version*, ed. Jean Pommier and Ga-
brielle Leleu (Paris, 1949), 224.

will be seen that *bleuâtre* sums up the nebulous and illusory content of Emma's lyrical thirsts. When Emma believes that Rodolphe will carry her off toward a "new country," she conjures up that future and coveted existence in this manner: "Cependant, sur l'immensité de cet avenir qu'elle se faisait apparaître, rien de particulier ne surgissait; les jours, tous magnifiques, se ressemblaient comme des flots; et cela se balançait à l'horizon, infini, harmonieux, *bleuâtre* et couvert de soleil" (201) 'However, in the immensity of this future that she conjured up, nothing specific stood out; the days, all magnificent, resembled one another like waves; and it all swayed on the horizon, infinite; harmonious, *bluish* and bathed in sunshine.'

Similarly, as Emma finds in her affair with Léon "all the platitudes of marriage," she imagines, even as she writes to her lover, another man, an ideal man composed from her memories, her headiest readings, her most lustful desirings: "Il habitait *la contrée bleuâtre* où les échelles de soie se balancent à des balcons, sous le souffle des fleurs, dans la clarté de la lune. Elle le sentait près d'elle, il allait venir et l'enlèverait tout entière dans un baiser" (297) 'He dwelled in *the bluish land* where silken ladders swung from balconies, swayed by flower-scented breezes, under the moonlight. She felt him near her; he was coming and would ravish her entire being in a single kiss.'

Contrée is here more suggestive and poetic than *pays* would be; it evokes something more expansive, something altogether grander: a domain, a realm. Coupled with *bleuâtre*, it becomes the perfect expression of the suave existence that Emma yearns for; it represents all that critics have variously termed *bovarysme* or the "tragedy of dreams." Blue is the textual sign that accompanies poetic reveries.[14] In the reader's first glimpse of Emma in her blue merino dress with three flounces, the color blue may

---

14. Martin Turnell briefly mentioned "the *pays bleu*, the land of Romantic love," in his "*Madame Bovary*," originally published in the *Sewanee Review*, LIV (1957), 531–50, and since reprinted in Raymond Giraud (ed.), *Flaubert: A Collection of Critical Essays* (Englewood Cliffs, N.J., 1964), 97–111 (see 106 for quotation). The same critic took note of Flaubert's "particular fondness for blue" in his *The Novel in France* (New York, 1958), 269. Earlier, D. L. Demorest, in *L'Expression figurée et symbolique dans l'oeuvre de Gustave Flaubert* (Paris, 1931), 431, had also mentioned "le pays bleu des rêves" 'the blue land of dreams.'

be unmotivated, without semantic weight, as may subsequent mentions of her blue silk cravat and her purchase of blue cashmere (86, 128).[15] She later finds desperately needed money in a roll of blue paper, sees Rodolphe leave Yonville in a blue tilbury (and later, after she has "forgotten" him, hopes to purchase such a tilbury for herself), and receives lace wrapped in blue paper from Lheureux (195, 212, 293). Yet, no significance necessarily attaches to these appearances of blue.

But the situation is quite different in one of the key scenes of the novel: Emma's seduction by Rodolphe. Emma wears a blue veil, and standing beside Rodolphe on a hill above Yonville, she contemplates a scene, as Jean Rousset has pointed out, that goes far beyond mere landscape description.[16]

> On était aux premiers jours d'octobre. Il y avait du *brouillard* sur la campagne. Des *vapeurs* s'allongeaient à l'horizon, entre le contour des collines; et d'autres se déchirant, montaient, se perdaient. Quelquefois, dans un écartement des *nuées*, sous un rayon de soleil, on apercevait au loin les toits d'Yonville, avec les jardins au bord de l'eau, les cours, les murs, et le clocher de l'église. Emma fermait à demi les paupières pour reconnaître sa maison, et jamais ce pauvre village où elle vivait ne lui avait semblé *si petit*. De la hauteur où ils étaient, toute la vallée paraissait un immense lac pâle, *s'évaporant* à l'air. (162)

> It was early in October. There was a *fog* over the countryside. *Vapors* extended toward the horizon, between the outlines of the hills; and others still, rent asunder, rose upward and disappeared. Sometimes, in a break in the *clouds*, beneath a ray of sunshine, the rooftops of Yonville could be seen in the distance, with the gardens at the water's edge, the yards, the walls, and the church steeple. Emma half closed her eyelids to recognize her house, and never had the poor village she lived in seemed *so small*. From the height where they stood, the whole valley looked like a huge pale lake, *evaporating* into the air.

The italicized key words in the passage suggest beyond their literal meaning a spiritual and poetic height Emma believes

15. Cashmere is an exotic, precious fabric, as attested by its value as an exchange object or fetish linking Mme Arnoux and Rosanette in *L'Education sentimentale*.

16. Jean Rousset, "*Madame Bovary* ou 'le livre sur rien,'" in Rousset, *Forme et signification* (Paris, 1962), 109–33, reprinted in Giraud (ed.), *Flaubert*, 112–31 (see esp. 124–25). Rousset notes that there is a corresponding "descent toward suicide" when Emma returns from seeing Rodolphe for the last time.

she has scaled. There can be no mistake as to the symbolic meaning of this passage, for a few pages later, as Emma deliciously and dramatically savors her new-found love, repeating to her mirror, "I have a lover! a lover!" Flaubert has composed a paragraph that transposes the descriptive landscape into a spiritual panorama.

Elle allait donc posséder enfin ces joies de l'amour, cette fièvre du bonheur dont elle avait désespéré. Ell entrait dans quelque chose de merveilleux où tout serait passion, extase, délire; une immensité *bleuâtre* l'entourait, les sommets du sentiment étincelaient sous sa pensée, et *l'existence ordinaire n'apparaissait qu'au loin, tout en bas, dans l'ombre, entre les intervalles de ces hauteurs.* (167)

At last she would possess those joys of love, that fever of happiness of which she had despaired. She was entering something marvelous where all would be passion, ecstasy, delirium; a *bluish* immensity enveloped her, the peaks of sentiment glittered beneath her thoughts, and *ordinary existence only appeared in the distance, down below, in the gaps amid these heights.*

Retrospectively, it is not hard to see that Emma's veil is not blue by chance and that the following notation, which comes just before Emma yields to Rodolphe, is not without suggestive traces of a poetic sort: "on distinguait son visage dans une transparence bleuâtre, comme si elle eût nagé sous des flots d'azur" (164) 'Her face appeared in a bluish transparency, as if she were swimming under waves of azure.'[17] Here blue, as everywhere in *Madame Bovary*, is an exorcising color and a sublimation of flat reality; it tenders hope for *suavités*, offers intimations of the fabulous. Its promises, as everyone knows, are false ones. And yet, Flaubert did not hesitate to write: "Je ne crois seulement qu'à l'éternité d'une chose, c'est à celle de l'*Illusion*, qui est la vraie vérité. Toutes les autres ne sont que relatives" 'I believe in the eternity of only one thing, that of *Illusion*, which is the real truth. All the others are merely relative.'[18]

"Seeing blue," then, stands for subjective vision or, in Kantian terms, *phenomena* rather than *noumena*. Flaubert seems con-

17. Demorest, *L'Expression figurée et symbolique*, 455, notes interesting variants for this particular image.
18. Flaubert, *Correspondance*, January 15, 1847.

sciously to have intended such a distortion, to judge by a highly interesting passage he finally suppressed. In it Emma, the night after the ball, surreptitiously visits a summer house on the grounds of La Vaubyessard and looks out at her surroundings from inside. What she sees is frighteningly transmogrified by the multicolored panes of the windows of the *maisonnette;* the panes are blue, yellow, green, and red.[19]

One cannot entirely dismiss minor touches of blue in the novel. It is not inappropriate that at least one mourner at Emma's funeral, Théodore, should stand out because of his blue suit, and it is certainly fitting that Léon, the more "poetic" of Emma's lovers, and Justin, the most "angelic," should have blue eyes (104, 132). This brings up the question of the color of Emma's eyes. They are first described in this manner: "Quoiqu'ils fussent bruns, ils semblaient noirs à cause des cils" (16) 'Although brown, they seemed black because of the eyelashes.' Later they are "noirs à l'ombre et bleu foncé au grand jour" (34) 'black in the shade and dark blue in broad daylight.' Then they are regularly black (51, 85, 133) until much later, when we read: "Ce fut comme le ciel, quand un coup de vent chasse les nuages L'amas de pensées tristes qui les assombrissaient parut se retirer de ses yeux *bleus;* tout son visage rayonna" (240) 'It was like the sky when a gust of wind blows away the clouds. The mass of sad, darkening thoughts seemed to lift from her *blue* eyes; her whole face shone.' B. F. Bart has called attention to this apparent contradiction, speculating that it is an instance of Flaubert's having imperfectly integrated his life sources (Louise Colet's eyes are known to have been blue, and Elisa Schlésinger's were probably black). He sees this as a discrepancy.[20]

For calling Flaubert "careless" on this score, Enid Starkie

19. Flaubert, *Madame Bovary, nouvelle version,* 215–16.
20. B. F. Bart, "Flaubert's Documentation Goes Awry, or, What Color Were Emma Bovary's Eyes?," *Romance Notes,* V (Spring, 1964), 138. Léon Bopp, *Commentaire sur Madame Bovary* (Neuchâtel, 1951), 368, simply says that her eyes have "changing hues." I might add that Emma's eyes are once again blue in a passage that has escaped Bart: "Et elle était ravissante à voir, avec son regard où tremblait une larme, comme l'eau d'un orage dans un calice *bleu*" (317) 'And she was lovely to see, with her eyes, where a tear was trembling like a storm in a *blue* chalice.'

earned (posthumously) the wrath of Geoffrey Braithwaite, the *Flaubertiste* narrator of Julian Barnes's ingenious novel, *Flaubert's Parrot*. In refutation of this charge against Flaubert, Braithwaite triumphantly produces a passage from the English translation of Maxime Du Camp's *Souvenirs littéraires* that describes "the woman on whom Emma Bovary was based." Her eyes, Du Camp wrote, were of "uncertain colour, green, gray, or blue, according to the light." This seems to absolve Flaubert in Braithwaite's mind, and he concludes in a cold fury, excoriating both Starkie and critics in general: "Dr. Starkie appears to have been serenely unaware of this enlightening passage. All in all, it seems a magisterial negligence towards a writer who must, one way and another, have paid a lot of her gas bills. Quite simply, it makes me furious. Now do you understand why I hate critics? I could try and describe to you the expression in my eyes at this moment; but they are far too discoloured with rage."[21]

In the end, Braithwaite thus joins Starkie and company as a naïvely mimetic reader of Flaubert. He is, if anything, even more concerned that the colors of Flaubert's models should be got "right" than she was, for his obsession—the main plot of *Flaubert's Parrot*—is to learn which of the two parrots claimed as the originals of Loulou is the "real" one. Which bird most conforms to Flaubert's description in "Un Coeur simple"? The problem, as he sees it, is that the parrot he thinks Flaubert borrowed first conforms less to the one described in the story. To settle the matter, Braithwaite visits a Flaubert scholar in Rouen, a M. Andrieu, who is the "secretary and oldest surviving member of the Société des Amis de Flaubert." Surely he can adjudicate. Alas, M. Andrieu explains that Flaubert was a writer "of the imagination" who would "alter a fact for the sake of a cadence," and concludes, to Braithwaite's consternation, "Why shouldn't he change the colours round if it sounded better?" Even after this explanation, Braithwaite remains the obstinate prisoner of the mimetic fallacy and fails to grasp the semiotic

21. Enid Starkie, *Flaubert: The Making of the Master* (London, 1967), 314; Julian Barnes, *Flaubert's Parrot* (London, 1984), 81.

thrust of his own baffled comment: "So you mean either of them could be the real one? Or, quite possibly, neither?"[22]

The "discrepancy" in the color of Emma's eyes, it should now be clear, can only be resolved once the reader is willing to abandon the level of mimesis for that of semiosis. In that case, the "ungrammaticality" of nature is exchanged for the coherence of semiotic coding. Blue is not a matter of pigmentation but of poesy: it is the color of reverie and fantasy. When Léon finds the courage to avow his past love for Emma ("Je vous ai bien aimée!" [240] 'I loved you dearly!'), Emma *envisages*—quite literally—a new possibility for happiness, a new promise of love. It is inevitable that blue, the idyllic color, should find its way into the passage to dispel her "sad thoughts."

Idyllic blue, Flaubertian coloration and nuance. But if all idylls are illusions, we should not be surprised to discover a double or ambiguous value in this color. And in *Madame Bovary* there are indeed idylls of life and idylls of death. The relationship between the two has been carefully prepared by Flaubert: the carriage of Emma and Léon's wild ride around Rouen is ominously described as "plus close qu'un tombeau et ballottée comme un navire" (250) 'closer shut than a tomb and tossed like a ship,' a phrase whose mortuary implications are clear enough and are rendered even more explicit by the subsequent description of Emma's bier advancing toward the grave like "une chaloupe qui tangue à chaque flot" (345) 'a launch pitching on every wave.' And in an earlier approach to death, as Emma contemplates sui-

22. In "The Follies of Writer Worship," *New York Times Book Review*, February 17, 1985, Barnes explains his longtime admiration of Flaubert and his desire to write a book on the master. Renouncing the temptation to do yet another biography, he follows Flaubert's injunction to take "revenge for the writer" against his detractors in the form of a novel. *Flaubert's Parrot* is thus as much a work of criticism as it is of fiction, and it allows for fictional "revenges" (such as that on Starkie) that would be in poor taste if written in a "serious" critical study. Barnes's article is about literary adulation, even literary fetishism (it begins, "I once owned a piece of Somerset Maugham's gate"), and here he acknowledges what his character can never fully reconcile himself to: "You may feel 'close' to a writer when you walk around his house and examine a lock of his hair, but the only time you are truly close is when you are reading words on the page. This is the only pure act."

cide after reading Rodolphe's farewell letter, "Il lui semblait que
. . . le plancher s'inclinait par le bout, à la manière d'*un vaisseau
qui tangue*. Elle se tenait tout au bord, presque suspendue, entourée d'un grand espace. Le *bleu* du ciel l'envahissait" (211) 'It
seemed to her that . . . the floor was tilting at the end, like *a
pitching boat*. She was standing right on the edge, almost hanging, surrounded by a vast space. The *blue* of the sky overwhelmed her.'[23] Emma seeks release, even in a form of the absolute that is closely related to perfect love, in death.

Sa chair *allégée* ne pensait plus, une autre vie commençait; il lui sembla
que son être, montant vers Dieu, allait *s'anéantir dans cet amour* comme un
encens allumé qui se dissipe en *vapeur*. On aspergea d'eau bénite les draps
du lit; le prêtre retira du saint ciboire la blanche hostie; et ce fut en
défaillant d'une joie céleste qu'elle avança les lèvres pour accepter le corps
du Sauveur qui se présentait. Les rideaux de son alcôve *se gonflaient molle-
ment*, autour d'elle, en façon de *nuées*, et les rayons des deux cierges
brûlant sur la commode lui parurent être des gloires éblouissantes. Alors
elle laissa retomber sa tête,[24] croyant entendre dans les espaces le chant
des harpes séraphiques et apercevoir en un ciel d'*azur*, sur un trône d'or,
au milieu des saints tenant des *palmes vertes*, Dieu le Père. (218–19)

Her flesh, *unburdened*, no longer thought; another life was beginning; it
seemed to her that her being, rising toward God, *would be annihilated in
that love* as a burning incense dissipates into *vapor*. The bedclothes were
sprinkled with holy water; the priest removed the white host from the
holy ciborium; and *swooning* with a celestial joy, she advanced her lips to
receive the body of the Saviour presented to her. The curtains of the alcove *billowed softly* round her like *clouds*, and the rays of the two candles
burning on the night table seemed like dazzling halos to her. Then she let
her head fall back, thinking she heard in space the music of seraphic
harps, and perceived in an *azure* sky, on a golden throne, in the midst of
saints holding *green palms*, God the Father.

If the reader will accept the interpretation that "an azure sky"
in this passage has symbolic overtones denied a purely descriptive blue sky, he has the right to demand a commensurate valua-

23. See also Demorest's comments in *L'Expression figurée et symbolique*, 456–57.
24. At La Vaubyessard "le vicomte, l'entraînant, disparut avec elle jusqu'au bout de
la galerie, où, haletante, elle faillit tomber, et, un instant, s'appuya la tête sur sa poitrine" (74) 'the viscount, drawing her along, disappeared with her to the end of the gal-
lery, where, panting, she nearly fell, and, for an instant, leaned her head on his chest.'

tion of the "green palms" in the last sentence quoted. This leads in turn to the question of the color of yet another character's eyes: the Blind Man's. The Blind Man, the most grotesque and frightening character in *Madame Bovary*, has been viewed as "an embodiment of corruption and meaningless death" and as the "macabre emblem of all physical love." He would indeed seem to incarnate the whole hideous comedy of life and death that Emma comes to realize. He suggests the misery and frailty of the human lot.[25] His role in *Madame Bovary* is that of an icono-graphic personage, a *blason* in the legend of which one might find (to evoke yet another motif) the biblical *Memento, homo, quia pulvis es et in pulverem reverteris*. He brings to Emma's life the lessons she might have learned from the neglected tour of the Rouen cathedral: "At least, leave by the north entrance," cried the verger, who was standing on the threshold, "to look at the *Resurrection*, the *Last Judgment*, *Paradise*, *King David*, and the *Damned* in the flames of hell!" (249, italics in original).

One of the most striking features in Flaubert's descriptions of the Blind Man is the hideous rolling of his "bluish pupils" (272); and yet some pages later he rolls in their bloody orbits his "greenish eyes" (306). And Emma, as if to placate this Cerberus-like herald of death, a monster, as Flaubert called him, grandly throws him her last five-franc coin.[26] This change would seem to be the accompaniment, within the semiotic coloring under discussion, of the author's love-religion-dreams-death analogy. Green may be the counterpart of blue, as inseparable from it as disenthrallment is from desire, as death from life. And it is certainly the Blind Man, "qui se dressait dans le ténèbres

---

25. Brombert, *The Novels of Flaubert*, 74. Levin, in *The Gates of Horn*, 265, called him a *memento mori*. Albert Thibaudet saw him as a "symbole de damnation" in *Gustave Flaubert* (Paris, 1922), 105. Demorest, *L'Expression figurée et symbolique*, 466, called him "l'incarnation de Némésis." The Blind Man, who, whipped by the coachman Hivert, falls screaming into the mud, looks forward to Félicité, another *figura* of suffering who is also whipped by a coachman while trudging along the road of life. The Blind Man—"c'est une compote où l'on ne distingue rien" 'He's an indistinguishable jelly' (Flaubert, *Correspondance*, September 19, 1855)—brings to mind another Flaubertian affinity with Brueghel's animal-vegetable *compotes*, such as the ghastly orbs in "The Parable of the Blind" and "The Beggars."

26. To hurry the burial ceremony in the church, Charles throws a five-franc coin to one of the cantors (343).

éternelles" 'rising up in the eternal darkness,' who chants the true funeral dirge of Emma Bovary, whose ritual "ashes to ashes, dust to dust," sends Emma into her final convulsion. His ditty reduces Emma's aspirations to their true dimensions and plunges her into nothingness.

> Pour amasser diligemment
> Les épis que la faux moissone,
> Ma Nanette va s'inclinant
> Vers le sillon qui nous les donne.[27]

> To gather diligently
> The stalks harvested by the scythe,
> My Nanette bends as she walks,
> Toward the furrow whence they come.

Emma's agony is attended by swirls of "vapeur bleuâtre" 'bluish vapor,' and her coffin makes its way toward the grave in the midst of "fumignons bleuâtres" 'bluish haze' hanging over iris-covered cottages (344). But her coffin is covered with a large swath of green velvet. The reader cannot but be reminded of Loulou, whose blues and greens Félicité associates with the Holy Ghost. The Spirit descends upon her deathbed in the form of a gigantic parrot whom she dimly perceives through a great "azure vapor." Félicité, too, experiences a "mystic sensuality" from those azure mists.

In retrospect, even the pious explanation of Emma's suicide, that she had mistaken the arsenic of the "blue jar" for sugar, assumes a meaning that escapes the characters' comprehension, just as does the irony of the *amabilem conjugem calcas!* on Emma's tomb.[28] The sweetness of the *contrée bleuâtre* has led Emma to a bitter end.

The blue country will always be associated with our chimerical aspirations and our ennui, which are forever inseparable, and in *Madame Bovary*, blue lends strength to the undertow

27. See Michael Riffaterre, "Flaubert's Presuppositions," *Diacritics*, XI (1981), 2–11, esp. 9–11.

28. William Bysshe Stein, in "*Madame Bovary* and Cupid Unmasked," *Sewanee Review*, LXXIII (Spring, 1965), 197–209, remarks that Homais' *capharnaüm* ironically "refers to the town where Christ performed numerous miracles of healing."

of sentiment that surreptitiously tugs at our sensibilities. The ironically placid surface conceals a current of sympathy, gently but firmly urging the reader to lose himself, with Emma, in what Flaubert termed *le grand bleu de la poésie—the grand blue of poetry.*[29]

29. Flaubert, *Correspondance*, March 27, 1853.

VII 🐦 Madame Arnoux's Coffret:

A Monumental Case

Readers have long recognized Flaubert's talent for investing material objects, especially those of the humblest sort, with a semantic potential that surpasses their status qua objects in the "real" world. A great deal of critical activity has indeed centered on the tracing out of such images, and it has culminated in the realization that taken together, they form a standard of Flaubertian literary practice or sign production. To illustrate with a single example drawn from Brombert's now classic study of Flaubert's novels, I cite the plaster priest in Emma's garden at Tostes, a sort of *pompier* art object that is seen to deteriorate slowly in the moral vacuum that follows Emma's exhilirating visit to the marquis' château and ball at La Vaubyessard. Time and weather chip away at it. We eventually learn that it has been smashed to bits during the move to Yonville. In relatively few pages, it has thus become "an ecclesiastical figure [that] parallels the gradual disintegration of their marriage."[1] The linking of statue and marriage is of course achieved through the simultaneous exposition of Emma's growing discontent, and thus, the

---

1. Victor Brombert, *The Novels of Flaubert* (Princeton, 1966), 48.

association is realized temporally, or if one prefers, in the linear or syntagmatic mode. Through a process of textual saturation (repetition being its instrument), the object, whose initial relation with Emma was strictly metonymical, is endowed with the independent signifying power of a metaphor.

An identical process could be traced in numerous other instances, and studies by Demorest and Bopp have devoted close attention to such details. One object whose textual density has yet to be satisfactorily catalogued and tracked in this manner is, in *L'Education sentimentale*, Mme Arnoux's *coffret*, or jewel case. It is but one of a number of artifacts that circulate from the Arnoux household to Rosanette's, from the "pure" milieu to the "impure" one, and that range from personal effects (such as umbrellas and cashmere wraps) and furnishings (such as the Dresden china chandelier) to political opinions and social alliances that are bartered like so many reprocessed items in an enormous rummage sale of the shop-soiled.

Frédéric Moreau's attachment to the coffret is extraordinary. It has nigh talismanic significance for him, such that its acquisition at a public auction by his intended, Mme Dambreuse, moves this protagonist, widely cited for his timidity and hesitation as a *velléitaire*, to take one of the few resolute and definitive actions of his existence, the renunciation of a brilliant marriage. As for the reader, his literary competence, brought into play by the very nature of the auction scene and the place it occupies in nineteenth-century European fiction, makes the experience of this episode a compelling and participatory one.

The coffret fits tightly into the scheme of profanation so repeatedly encoded into the semiotic structure of the novel. Initially mentioned on the occasion of Frédéric's first invitation to the Arnoux apartment, the "coffret à fermoirs d'argent" 'jewel box with silver clasps' stands on the mantelpiece beside a clock; it is thus indexed as an object of bourgeois respectability and standing that Flaubert might have chosen instead to metaphorize, as Zola was to do with Gervaise and Lantier's clock and savings-account passbook in *L'Assommoir*. The coffret is located in the boudoir, described as "a quiet, respectable, and intimate place, all at the same time."[2] It is apparently a recent gift from Arnoux, for after dinner Mme Arnoux fetches it to show her husband's guests, and developments would seem to mark it as an image of conjugal felicity, much like the plaster priest: "C'était un cadeau de son mari, un ouvrage de la Renaissance. Les amis d'Arnoux la complimentèrent, sa femme le remerciait; il fut pris d'attendrissement et lui donna devant le monde un baiser"(48) 'It was a gift from her husband, a Renaissance work. Arnoux's friends complimented her, his wife thanked him; he was overcome with tenderness and gave her a kiss in front of them all.'

Yet, the box is not to be constituted as a sign of marital fidelity, for it is from this same silver box that Mme Arnoux later produces the incriminating bill for the cashmere that finally confutes—at least momentarily—even the mendacious and adulterous Arnoux. In the meantime a coffret is part of the "Venetian" get-up that Pellerin imagines for his portrait of Rosanette. It was to be ivory rather than silver, and from it would issue a stream of golden sequins, indices of riches or prostitution. In the executed version, Rosanette holds a purse, which has the same semantic value—sex and money (151, 235). The coffret is only one of the several links joining Rosanette and Mme Arnoux, the pure and the impure, so closely do degradation and ideality coexist in Flaubert's universe.

Later the "chased silver box" makes a key appearance in Rosanette's apartment, where Frédéric is scandalized to discover it.

Il y avait sur la table, entre un vase plein de cartes de visite et une écritoire, un coffret d'argent ciselé. C'était celui de Mme Arnoux! Alors, il éprouva un attendrissement, et en même temps comme le scandale d'une profanation. Il avait envie d'y porter les mains, de l'ouvrir. Il eut peur d'être aperçu, et s'en alla. (260)

On the table, between a bowl full of visiting cards and a writing stand, was a chased silver box. It was Mme Arnoux's! Then he felt tenderness, and at the same time something like the scandal of a profanation. He

---

2. Gustave Flaubert, *L'Education sentimentale*, ed. Edouard Maynial (Paris, 1964), 46. All page references in the text are to this edition.

wanted to put his hands on it, to open it. He was afraid of being seen, and left.

Here the coffret's status is quasi-metaphorical. It is a material extension of Mme Arnoux's personal orbit, and Frédéric's desire to touch it (a phrasing that does not quite do justice to "d'y porter les mains") signals its "standing for" the physical person of Mme Arnoux. The intensity of Frédéric's reaction is indicated by the abrupt shift to free indirect discourse with an exclamation point and the term *profanation*. The expression "y porter les mains" is sexually suggestive, as are his shame and fear of exposure, the very sentiments that had restrained him from "putting his hands on" Rosanette a scant fifteen lines earlier.[3]

The sacred nature of the objects thus associated with the loved one explains their status as relics and thus their potential for involvement in a curiously ambiguous rite of both sanctification and profanation. When Mme Dambreuse drags Frédéric to the sale of the Arnoux's household goods, the public handling of her most intimate garments—"skirts, shawls, handkerchiefs, and even chemises were being passed from hand to hand"—seems like a sharing out of relics, an atrocity that makes him conceive of her as if she were dead, "as if he had seen crows tearing at her corpse" (413).[4] Her box, when it comes up for sale, is thus associated with death.

The sale at public auction of an indebted or dead person's goods is a fairly common scene in nineteenth-century fiction. It is called being "sold up" in the English novel, and there are examples of it in Thackeray (*Vanity Fair*), Hardy (*Tess of the d'Urbervilles*, *The Mayor of Casterbridge*), and George Eliot (*The Mill on the Floss*). It is the sequel to bankruptcy, which in turn is

3. Here we can cite Freud's "Dora" case. In Dora's puzzling dream Freud saw that the jewel box was a sexual symbol: "The box—*Dose, Pyxis*—, like the reticule and the jewel-case, was once again only a substitute for the shell of Venus, for the female genitals." "Fragment of an Analysis of a Case of Hysteria (1905 [1901])," in *The Standard Edition of the Complete Psychological Works of Sigmund Freud* (24 vols.; London, 1953–74), VII 77.

4. In *Madame Bovary*, as the *huissier* and his two witnesses examine Emma's personal effects, she has the impression that it is her existence, "like a corpse for autopsy," that is laid out for inspection. Gustave Flaubert, *Madame Bovary*, ed. Claudine Gothot-Mersch (Paris, 1971), 301.

the ultimate bourgeois dishonor. Readers of Balzac remember old Grandet's pitiless characterization of his nephew's disgrace upon finding himself the son of a man who has gone bankrupt: "To go bankrupt is to commit the most dishonorable action among all those that can dishonor mankind." They remember also César Birotteau's epic climb back to integral restitution of his debts and thus respectability. But the disgrace is not only bourgeois; Barbey d'Aurevilly described the public auction of Beau Brummell's furniture in his *Du Dandysme et de George Brummell*.

Tous voulaient . . . ces reliques précieuses d'un luxe épuisé, ces objets consacrés par le goût d'un homme, ces frêles choses fungibles, touchées et à moitié usées par Brummell. Ce qui fut payé le plus cher par cette société opulente . . . fut précisément ce qui avait le moins de valeur en soi, les babioles.[5]

Everyone wanted . . . those precious relics of an exhausted extravagance, those objects consecrated by one man's taste, those frail, fungible things, touched and half worn out by Brummell. What was paid most dearly by that opulent society . . . was precisely what had the least intrinsic value, the knickknacks.

And Barbey goes on to mention Brummell's collection of *tabatières*, snuffboxes, objects physically quite similar to Mme Arnoux's coffret.

As I have already observed, few authors are so capable of poetizing objects as Flaubert, of producing the sheer evocative power with which he invests his inventories of things from the past, so that they read like litanies of heartbreak.[6] They range from Charles's veneration of the dead Emma's gowns to Félicité's poor collection of object-memories to the naming of the contents as they are sold one by one—a carpet, a screen, a wing

5. Barbey d'Aurevilly, "Du dandysme et de Georges Brummell," in *Œuvres Romanesques Complètes*, ed. Jacques Petit (2 vols.; Paris, 1972), II, 706.
6. By "poetizing an object," I mean bestowing aesthetic energy upon it. As Mary Louise Pratt has pointed out, however, such usage is contestable to the extent that it is metaphorical, that is, based on the *langue/parole* distinction formulated by Tomashevsky and Eichenbaum to oppose poetic to nonpoetic ("everyday") language. I use *poetic* simply to designate that which *contextually* is no longer a "mot de la tribu." See Mary Louise Pratt, *Toward a Speech Act Theory of Literary Discourse* (Bloomington, 1977), esp. Ch. 1, "The 'Poetic Language' Fallacy."

chair—of Mme Arnoux's bedroom. And they are often circum-scribed by closed spaces suggesting sanctuaries for worship of the departed presence: Emma's *cabinet de toilette*, where Charles "closed himself in" to think of Emma; Félicité's garret bedroom, crowded with her pathetic souvenirs, where she prays before the stuffed parrot, Loulou; and the *hôtel des commissaires-priseurs*, the auction house, where the Arnoux household goods are stacked in one of its apartments "at the end of the corridor, to-ward a room full of people." It can be objected that because of the phrase "full of people," this is no place for solitary devo-tions. But these rude presences are precisely what transform the scene into a profanation of the sanctuary, a sacrilege and a soiling of the ideal. And it might be pointed out that Charles and Félicité mourn their dead ones, whereas Mme Arnoux is quite alive. Yet, the language of the text is couched in the death code: "reliques," "cadavre," "plume cassée," "torpeur funèbre," "dissolution." Its mechanism operates like a hyperbolization of absence, as if she were effectively dead.

It is within this context that the coffret is valorized as perhaps the sole remaining metonym of privacy, of a cult not yet opened to the *profanum vulgus*. It is no doubt this that makes Frédéric react so vehemently to Mme Dambreuse's apparently sudden decision to bid for it: "'Tiens! je vais l'acheter'" 'You know, I'm going to buy it.' And just as Frédéric seeks to defend from ex-posure this last unexposed relic of his love—for its *fermoirs d'argent* ('silver clasps,' but deriving from *fermer* 'to close') seem to shut up from view some secret of her existence—so Mme Dambreuse seems equally determined to bare the secret, to ex-pose and so to humiliate.

—"Quelle singulière idée!" dit Frédéric.
—"Cela vous fâche?"
—"Non! Mais que peut-on faire de ce bibelot?"
—"Qui sait? y mettre des lettres d'amour, peut-être!"
Elle eut un regard qui rendait l'allusion fort claire. (414–15)

"What an odd idea!" said Frédéric.
"Does it bother you?"
"No! But what can this trinket be used for?"

"Who knows? for love letters, maybe!"
Her look made the allusion quite clear.

Mme Dambreuse not only outbids all competitors for the coffret, but she doubly appropriates it by stuffing it deep into her muff and guiltily throws herself into her carriage "like a thief." Thus, Pierre Cogny's classification of the "coffret à fermoirs *d'argent*" (his italics) as an "index of wealth" is surely a mistaken emphasis, for a retroactive reading marks it otherwise.[7] Somewhat like the *zaïmph* of *Salammbô*, it embodies the tangible form of an absence, an enigmatic cult, an "imagined." And like the *zaïmph*, it is associated with the veneration of a kind of goddess and is stolen ("like a thief") by an outsider.

If the reader adheres without dissent to the great significance that Frédéric attaches to the coffret, this is no doubt largely an effect of the way the text establishes the object's pertinence syntagmatically. It is linked with the three most important women in Frédéric's life (Mme Arnoux, Rosanette, and now Mme Dambreuse) and endowed with great motivational power. Indeed, Rosanette's sudden and weakly motivated appearance at the auction (she presumably comes to gloat over Mme Arnoux's downfall) seems to be an index of the coffret's actualizing powers, as if the object conjured up her presence through a mnemotechnical effect. As previously noted, the coffret precipitates Frédéric's break with Mme Dambreuse and thus all possibility of leading the luxurious Parisian existence to which he had previously aspired. This is a revolutionary action, as indicated structurally by its coincidence with the prince-président's coup d'état, which underscores Flaubert's textual pinning of story to History (a kind of "hisStory"). The coffret has undergone that process whereby metonym becomes metaphor through textual determination.

A textual sign, the coffret possesses an additional, indwelling significance that is achieved through overdetermination, that is, through embedded allusions and references that make demands upon the reader's competence and that check or grasp the reader's

---

7. Pierre Cogny, *L'Education sentimentale de Flaubert: Le monde en creux* (Paris, 1975), 148.

attention even at considerable temporal remove from the intertexts to which it gestures. Michael Riffaterre explains *monumentality* as an effect of overdetermination in this way:

The functions of overdetermination are three: to make mimesis possible;
to make literary discourse exemplary by lending it the authority of multiple motivations for each word used; and to compensate for the catachresis. The first two functions are observable in literature in general, the
last only in poetic discourse. The three together confer upon the literary
text its monumentality: it is so well built and rests upon so many intricate
relationships that it is relatively impervious to change and deterioration of
the linguistic code. Because of the complexity of its structures and the
multiple motivations of its words, the text's hold on the reader's attention
is so strong that even his absent-mindedness or, in later eras, his estrangement from the esthetic reflected in the poem or its genre, cannot quite
obliterate the poem's features or their power to control his decoding.[8]

Thus, in addition to being a unity formal and semantic, the
literary monument is *transformal*. Its seeming naturalness is paradoxical, for this effect is based on nothing more than its reference to prior artifacts and signifying systems that appear to di-
minish its arbitrariness by "justifying" it, by conferring upon it
a paternity of sorts and thus a legitimacy.[9]

While these insights cannot and should not be deployed in a
misguided attempt to "explain" the density of Flaubert's novel—
happily, texts resist theory—these categories can be adapted
and tested in an attempt to account for the signifying power of
the auction scene. To focus on its paradigms is to account, at
least in part, for those subsurface dimensions of the work that
can only be retrieved through literary competence: the accumulation of reading experience that taps the historically collateral
layers of a text. And the weight and wealth of plausible intertexts for the auction scene of *L'Education sentimentale* are im-
pressive indeed.

A first intertext is Dumas fils' novel version of *La Dame aux
camélias* (1848). This work might well have been forgotten had it
not been for the astounding success achieved by the play ver-

8. Michael Riffaterre, *Semiotics of Poetry* (Bloomington, 1978), 21–22.
9. See Michael Riffaterre, "Modèles de la phrase littéraire," in Riffaterre, *La Production du texte* (Paris, 1979), 49.

sion of 1852 (and its notoriety for having been banned in 1851). The subject of both novel and play, prostitution and society, would have been enough to interest Flaubert, and the novel begins with an auction that offers a number of points touching upon Flaubert's scene.[10] In Dumas fils we have an intradiegetic narrator who himself sees in the opening chapter a placard announcing the public sale of furniture and *objets de curiosité*, a sale that is to take place "après décès" of the owner, that is, to satisfy the debts of the dead Marguerite Gautier. Prior to the sale the goods are on public display in Marguerite's home, and the narrator examines them there in the company of "pure" women: "Celle chez qui je me trouvais était morte: les femmes les plus vertueuses pouvaient donc pénétrer jusque dans sa chambre. La mort avait purifié l'air de ce cloaque superbe" 'The woman whose home I was in was dead: the most virtuous women could therefore penetrate even into her bedroom. Death had purified the air of this magnificent sewer.' Also common to the two scenes is the inventory, an indispensable component of the *vente aux enchères*. Thus Dumas fils: rosewood furniture, Sèvres vases, fine China, satins, velvets, laces. Curiosities from the private rooms ("chambre" and "cabinet de toilette") are also on view. The personal items in Dumas fils—"Dresses, cashmeres, jewels"—find lexical homologues in Flaubert, and there is the striking copresence of the strumpet and the society lady on auction day itself, treated by Dumas fils in Chapter 3: "Madame la duchesse de F . . . coudoyait mademoiselle A . . ., une des plus tristes épreuves de nos courtisanes modernes; madame la marquise de T . . . hésitait pour acheter un meuble sur lequel enchérissait madame D . . ., la femme adultère, la plus élégante et la plus connue de notre époque" 'Madame the Duchess of F—— rubbed elbows with Mademoiselle A——, one of the lowest examples of our modern-day courtesans; Madame the Marquise of T—— hesitated to buy a piece of furniture bid on by Madame D——, the most elegant and notorious adulteress of our times.'

10. There are a few generally unflattering references to Dumas fils in Flaubert's correspondence.

The last named has both a description and an initial that could be applied to Frédéric's companion. Finally, the narrator of *La Dame aux camélias* engages in a spirited bidding for a copy, *doré sur tranche*, of *Manon Lescaut* (a rather obvious embedded intratextual allusion to its owner, Marguerite Gautier). The narrator tops all competitors with a jump to a round and handsome bid of a hundred francs (Mme Dambreuse made a similar stopping bid of a thousand francs), spurred on by the auctioneer's announcement "Il y a quelque chose d'écrit sur la première page" 'There is something written on the first page.' What messages might the closed objects contain, what essential *texts* of their owners' existence? Both bidders thus dramatize the desire to *possess* the secret of the dead woman, to penetrate the private space of the letter-enigma.

But what is the explanation for this correlation, apparently effected through juxtaposition, between the boxlike object and the woman, and further, between them and death?

In a memorable essay that begins with a scene from Shakespeare, Freud writes of the three caskets that Portia's suitors are to choose among in *The Merchant of Venice* that "if what we were concerned with here were a dream, it would occur to us at once that caskets are also women, symbols of what is essential in woman, and therefore of woman herself—like coffers, boxes, cases, baskets, and so on."[11] He recognizes a similar pattern in the three daughters of *King Lear*, and further observes that Cordelia's silence, her dumbness at a crucial moment, is an attribute or rather a symbolic equivalent of death. Freud undertakes to explain this filiation between the treasured woman and death by analyzing a number of related sister myths in which the third sister stands for death—"the Fates, the Moerae, the Parcae and the Norns, the third of whom is called Atropos, the inexorable." The essay then turns to explaining the psychological process whereby death, in the exercise of man's imaginative activity, is made equivalent to love. Freud does not mention Flaubert, but he could easily have referred to the three-box motif in *Madame*

11. Sigmund Freud, "The Theme of the Three Caskets," in *Complete Psychological Works of Freud*, XII, 291–301.

Bovary, in which Emma's body is encased in three coffins: one of oak, one of mahogany, one of lead. (Lead, incidentally, was the box the fortunate Bassanio chose in Shakespeare.)

If the profferred box (the auction being a variation of the matrix concept of bartered love) holds such a large place in the fictions created by the Western imagination, then we should certainly seek instances of it in Balzac. Although Flaubert's opinion of the great novelist of the Romantic era declined with the passage of time, the example of Balzac was unavoidable for any practicing novelist of Flaubert's time, whether French or not. At least three Balzacian texts, to varying degrees, suggest themselves as overdeterminers of the auction scene. The first is *La Peau de chagrin*, with its fantastic ascent through the floors of the antiquarian's shop, during the course of which Raphaël de Valentin (who is also taken for a thief) traverses a jumble of apparently unrelated objects that constitutes an archaeology of human memory.[12] Raphaël concludes a Faustian pact with a Mephistopheles-like personage who is presented as a death figure: "La robe ensevelissait le corps comme dans un vaste linceul, et ne permettait de voir d'autre forme humaine qu'un visage étroit et pâle" 'The robe entombed his body as if in an enormous shroud and of the human form allowed only a glimpse of a narrow, ashen face.'

Similarly, in *L'Education sentimentale* the protagonists pass amid "washbasins with missing bowls, wood from armchairs, old baskets, porcelain shards, empty bottles, mattresses," and the impression of space, of distance traveled, is accentuated by means of phrases marking their progress: "They went up the stairs. . . . Mme Dambreuse tried to go down. . . . and she led him to the end of the corridor, toward a room full of people" (412–13). Both itineraries could ultimately be traced to the ancient topos of the descent into the underworld, the visit to the realm of the dead or the damned, as in Virgil or Dante.

In *Eugénie Grandet*, Charles Grandet entrusts to Eugénie's safekeeping a gold box containing his parents' portraits, "une

---

12. The apparent disorder is in reality highly ordered. See Chapter I.

chose qui m'est aussi précieuse que la vie. Cette boîte est un présent de ma mère" 'a thing as precious to me as life. This box is a present from my mother.' *Caisse, nécessaire, coffre,* and *coffret* are other terms used by Balzac to designate this object, which, closed away from sight in a great chest near Eugénie's empty money purse, becomes the tangible sign of her betrothal to her cousin. (I pass over the inverted variation of bartered love here.) Eugénie defends it from her father's predations by threatening suicide and is shocked when Charles, many years later, asks her to have it returned by coach: "—'By coach!' said Eugénie. 'A thing I'd have given my life a thousand times for!'" [13]

A more narrowly focused model episode in *Le Père Goriot* might also serve. There we find another drastic change in social condition, and it is coded in the same mortuary lexicon. This being Balzac, a number of the lexical items forming the code consist of allusions to history or mythology. The situation is briefly this: betrayed by her faithless lover, Mme de Beauséant, cynosure of the Faubourg Saint-Germain, will give one last brilliant ball that will constitute her stoic farewell to the beau monde. All her guests will know of her grief, but she will not allow her so-called friends the slightest glimpse of her suffering: "Personne ne pouvait lire dans son âme. Vous eussiez dit d'une Niobé de marbre. . . . Les plus insensibles l'admirèrent, comme les jeunes Romaines applaudissaient le gladiateur qui savait sourire en expirant" 'No one could read in her heart. She looked like a marble Niobe. . . . The most insensitive people admired her, as young Roman women used to applaud the glad-iator who could smile as he was dying.' In a final private inter-view with his *cousine*, Rastignac gives her a "cassette en cèdre" 'cedar box' containing her love letters to Adjuda-Pinto, which she throws into the fire, announcing "They're dancing! They all came right on time, but death will come late. . . . At five this morning I'll be leaving to bury myself deep in Normandy." [14]

She then chooses to make Rastignac a gift of an object that is

13. Honoré de Balzac, *Eugénie Grandet*, ed. P.-G. Castex (Paris, 1965), 161, 242. Flaubert mentions rereading *Eugénie Grandet* in a letter of 1854 to Louis Bouilhet.

14. Honoré de Balzac, *Le Père Goriot*, ed. P.-G. Castex (Paris, 1960), 278–80.

physically similar to the one she has just received from him and disposed of—a presumably empty coffret.

> "Je penserai souvent à vous. . . . Je souhaite que vous songiez quelquefois à moi. Tenez, dit-elle en jetant les yeux autour d'elle, voici le coffret où je mettais mes gants. Toutes les fois que j'en ai pris avant d'aller au bal ou au spectacle, je me sentais belle, parce que j'étais heureuse, et je n'y touchais que pour y laisser quelque pensée gracieuse: il y a beaucoup de moi là-dedans, il y a toute une madame de Beauséant qui n'est plus. Acceptez-le."[15]

> "I shall think of you often. . . . I want you to think of me sometimes. Here," she said glancing around her, "take this box where I used to put my gloves. Every time I took out a pair before going to the ball or the theater, I felt pretty, because I was happy, and I only left the imprint of gracious thoughts on it. There is a lot of me in there, there's a whole Madame de Beauséant who no longer exists. Accept it."

Mme de Beauséant's last sentence renders explicit a metaphoric status that Mme Arnoux's coffret only acquires through the reader's work, particularly through the retroactive constructing of that equivalence.

It is worth observing that the coffret is not the only point of contact with Balzac in *L'Education sentimentale*. As the youths plot their rise to fame and fortune, Rastignac and the *Comédie humaine* are explicitly mentioned as models of social success. The youthful friends urge one another to emulate the successful ways of Rastignac and fervently wish for "des amours de princesses dans des boudoirs de satin, ou de fulgurantes orgies avec des courtisanes illustres" (13) 'affairs with princesses in satin covered boudoirs, or blazing orgies with celebrated courtesans,' the latter being Rastignac-like aspirations. Such allusions must ultimately be considered ironic, however, for Frédéric is obviously no Rastignac, a point that is made almost parodically clear when Frédéric accompanies M. Dambreuse's funeral procession to the heights of the Père Lachaise cemetery. In similar circumstances, and from the same lofty position at the conclusion of *Père Goriot*, Rastignac had gazed at the panorama of Paris

15. *Ibid.*, 280.

spread beneath him, and issued his emphatic challenge to society: "A nous deux, maintenant!" 'And now, it's between the two of us!' And he marched off to dinner with a banker's wife as the first step in the implementation of Mme de Beauséant's advice to him to use women to further his career. Frédéric is too delicate, too passive ever to entertain the thoughts of a parvenu. During the burial ceremony, his gaze strays randomly over various curiosities afforded by the great height—green treetops seen from above, pumping engine smokestacks, the great city itself: "Frédéric put admirer le paysage pendant qu'on prononçait les discours" (382–83) 'During the speeches Frédéric was able to admire the view.'

Rastignac's view had likened Paris to a great beehive from which he would greedily "pump the honey"; Frédéric's view is of mechanical pumps. The degree of effort (or lack thereof) represented by the finality of the past definite formation *put admirer* points to a deliberate subversion or ironic reinscription of the famous Balzacian antecedent. Yet, the very convergence of Balzacian and Flaubertian texts, however ironic, permits us to observe the absence of memory, of nostalgia, without which Balzac can never serve as proper model for that intertextual stiffening that goes into the building of monumentality. Let us briefly contrast Balzac and Flaubert on this point, then situate memory, the indispensable condition for overdetermination, within the Flaubert corpus.

Balzac is the author of anticipation—Flaubert, of retrospection. Rastignac will have little time to look *back* upon his life; all his efforts move him forward. Frédéric, on the other hand, only moves forward in time the better to remember and to evoke the past. "Old before his time" is a phrase that, rather than a regret, sums up a longed for, precious state of preservation. During his chaste summer idyll with Mme Arnoux in Auteuil, the Platonic lovers evoke their past: "Il lui rappelait d'insignifiants détails, la couleur de sa robe à telle époque, quelle personne un jour était survenue, ce qu'elle avait dit une autre fois; et elle répondait tout émerveillée: —Oui, je me rappelle!" (272) 'He reminded her of insignificant details: the color of her dress on a particular day, which person had unexpectedly arrived one day, what she had said another time, and in amazement she would reply— Yes, I remember!' During their last meeting the lovers tell one another "about their old days," and Mme Arnoux "rapturously accepted these adorations of the woman she no longer was." She exclaims, in a verbal aspect that Brombert called the very tense of "anticipated retrospection,"[16] "N'importe, nous nous serons bien aimés" 'Never mind, we shall have loved one another well.' And in the final chapter of the book Frédéric and Deslauriers, reconciled and reunited once again, pass their time "exhuming their youth" and repeating at every phrase, "Do you remember?"

Frédéric is thus the man of memory, of *souvenir.* He is himself the genetic descendant and projection of the narrator of another youthful text, *Novembre,* where on the first page we read: "J'ai savouré longuement ma vie perdue. . . . J'ai repassé lentement dans toutes les choses de ma vie. . . . J'ai tout revu, comme un homme qui visite les catacombes et qui regarde lentement, des deux côtés, des morts rangés après des morts" 'I've savored my lost youth at length. . . . I've slowly gone over all the things of my life. . . . I've seen everything again, as a man who visits the catacombs and slowly looks, on both sides, at dead after dead.'

With the mention of catacombs we come again to the image of the closed, holy, sepulchral space that preserves memory. According to Jean Bruneau, Flaubert composed *Novembre* most likely between 1840 and 1842.[17] Twelve years later, in the same letter where he spoke to Louise Colet of the famous desire to write "a book about nothing" (he had been at work on *Madame Bovary* for almost four months), Flaubert used remarkably similar language to ask his mistress about the remembrance of feelings.

Sonde-toi bien: y a-t-il un sentiment que tu aies eu qui soit disparu? Non, tout reste, n'est-ce pas? tout. Les momies que l'on a dans le cœur ne tom-

16. Brombert, *The Novels of Flaubert,* 153.
17. Jean Bruneau, *Les Débuts littéraires de Gustave Flaubert (1831–1845)* (Paris, 1962), 311.

bent jamais en poussière et, quand on penche la tête par le soupirail, on les voit en bas, qui vous regardent avec leurs yeux ouverts, immobiles.[18]

Probe into the past: is there one feeling you've had that has disappeared? No, everything is there, isn't it? Everything. The mummies in our hearts never fall into dust, and when you lean your head over, you can see them down below, looking at you with their open, unmoving eyes.

To return to the so appropriately titled *Novembre*, the passage continues:

A compter les années cependant, il n'y a pas longtemps que je suis né, mais j'ai à moi des souvenirs nombreux dont je me sens accablé, comme le sont les vieillards de tous les jours qu'ils ont vécus; *il me semble quelquefois que j'ai duré pendant des siècles, et que mon être renferme les débris de mille existences passées* (italics added).

To count by the years, however, it's not long since I was born, but I feel overwhelmed by all my many memories, as old men are by the days of their lives; *sometimes it seems to me that I have endured for centuries, and that my being encloses the remains of a thousand past existences* (italics added).

The "Egyptian" chords of an ancient existence, remembered beyond death, are unmistakably struck here with the references to catacombs, mummies, and unending duration.

In another movement of frustrated anticipation of memory, the narrator writes of his desire to fall in love: "Je me disais 'C'est celle-là que j'aime'; mais *le souvenir que j'aurais voulu en garder s'appâlissait et s'effaçait au lieu de grandir*" (italics added) 'I would say to myself, she's the one I love; but *the memory I would have liked to keep of her* paled and faded instead of growing.' As further proof of the profound ties binding *Novembre* to *L'Education sentimentale*, we can cite this passage, which it would seem legitimate to call an *avant-texte* of the mature work: "Marie ne me parla plus. . . . Elle songeait peut-être à l'amant absent. Il y a un instant, dans le départ où, *par anticipation de tristesse*, la personne aimée n'est déjà plus avec vous" (italics added) 'Marie spoke no more. . . . Perhaps she was thinking of the absent lover. There comes a moment in separations when, *in anticipa-*

<hr>

18. Gustave Flaubert, *Correspondance*, ed. Jean Bruneau (Paris, 1980), January 16, 1852.

tion of sadness, the loved one is no longer with you.' In the last sentence, virtually the only difference between the phrasing of the early 1840s and the text of nearly thirty years later is the deletion of the italicized words (see *L'Education sentimentale*, 423). Smarh had already told Satan: "J'ai en moi le souvenir de dix existences passées" and "J'ai comme, dans mon âme, les débris de vingt mondes" 'The meaning of ten past existences is in me' and 'I have, in my soul, something akin to the debris of twenty worlds.'[19]

The foregoing models constitute, to my mind, plausible convergences with the auction of Mme Arnoux's coffret. I shall now attempt to clinch my point by producing a text that, in addition to those features common to Balzac and Dumas fils, will account for memory and for other elements in the auction scene, particularly the inventory of objects that is obligatory in the descriptive system of the auction sale. As we have seen, this is touched upon in *La Dame aux camélias*, but the affiche is not nearly as fulsome, or rather pathetic and pitiless, as the one posted on the Arnoux's door: "Vente d'un riche mobilier, consistant en batterie de cuisine, linge de corps et de table, chemises, dentelles, jupons, pantalons, cachemires français et de l'Inde, piano d'Erard, deux bahuts de chêne Renaissance, miroirs de Venise, poteries de Chine et du Japon" (409–10) 'Sale of fine furnishings, consisting of kitchen utensils, table and personal linen, shirts, laces, skirts, trousers, French and Indian cashmeres, Erard piano, two Renaissance oak chests, Venetian mirrors, Chinese and Japanese pottery.' Such a text, stylistically enumerative, must also account for the seemingly aberrant but crucial detail in Flaubert's scene; the problematic "death" of Mme Arnoux. For though the lady is quite *alive*, and threatened not by death but with enforced withdrawal to the provinces (much like Mme de Beauséant's voluntary exile), Frédéric inexplicably speaks of her as if she were dead. This is the catachresis, the *scordatura* of Flaubert's fictional composition. It is

19. Gustave Flaubert, *Œuvres Complètes*, Collection L'Intégrale (2 vols.; Paris, 1964), I, 208, 209.

this departure from the mimetic grammar of the episode (and the text as a whole, for she is not dead in this scene, nor does she later die in the course of the story) that signals the presence of an interference, an intertext whose compelling features briefly distort the fictional facts. This constitutes an "ungrammaticality," here a contradiction on the level of plot consistency that can only be explained by the text's adherence to a subsurface intertext. And while this is certainly the most important requirement in establishing overdetermination, the most convincing aspect should be that Flaubert himself confirmed his reading and high esteem of this resolving intertext.

The conditions can be satisfied by turning to a letter dated July 13, 1857 in the *Correspondance*. It is to Baudelaire; in it Flaubert enthusiastically expresses his admiration for *Les Fleurs du mal*, having devoured Baudelaire's presentation copy "comme une cuisinière fait d'un feuilleton" 'the way a scullery maid does an installment novel.' Flaubert praises eleven poems by name or number and requotes a few verses that had struck him. He singles out two poems for special praise: "La Beauté" (a work of the "highest value" for him) and "'Spleen' (p. 140), qui m'a nuvré, tant c'est juste de couleur! Ah! vous comprenez l'embêtement de l'existence, vous! Vous pouvez vous vanter de cela, sans orgueil" '"Spleen" (p. 140), which upset me, so just is its color! Ah! you understand the tedium of existence, you do! You can brag of it, with no pride.'

But to which of the "Spleen" poems does Flaubert refer? It would best suit the argument of this essay were the "Spleen" referred to turn out to be number LXXVI, the famous "J'ai plus de souvenirs que si j'avais mille ans" 'I have more memories than if I had lived a thousand years,' a poem rich in evocations of objects and memory and containing a long series of variations on the box matrix as well as Egyptian imagery. Luckily, Flaubert has provided us with a precise reference: "p. 140." On that page of the original edition of *Les Fleurs du mal*, published by Poulet-Malassis in 1857, appears this very poem, the second of the four bearing the title "Spleen." "Spleen" LXXVI (the

1857 numbering was LX) is displayed in a two-page layout, page 140 being a left-hand page and page 141 being a right-hand page. Thus, the reader can take in the entire poem without turning the page and without parts of the preceding or following poem to distract his attention. (There is thus absolutely no doubt about which of the "Spleen" poems had impressed Flaubert.) This typographical siting is true of all the "Spleen" poems and is the format found in forty-seven of the original one hundred pieces. Of the eleven poems mentioned by Flaubert, six are so disposed, including "La Beauté." Rather generous leading—blank spacing—divides the poem into three parts: the striking and, as we have seen, "Flaubertian" first line (inasmuch as it could be said to echo *Novembre*), then lines 2–14, and finally lines 15–24. The last section is without a doubt the one Flaubert praises in his references to Baudelaire's understanding of the "tedium of existence," for it contains the famous line "L'ennui, fruit de la morne incuriosité." Other lines touch upon Flaubertian themes of petrification and massivity and evoke North African settings dear to the writer of *Salammbô* and *La Tentation de Saint-Antoine.*

> —Désormais tu n'es plus, ô matière vivante!
> Qu'un granit entouré d'une vague épouvante,
> Assoupi dans le fond d'un Saharah brumeux;
>
> —Hereafter, O living matter, you are no more!
> Than granite surrounded by a nameless fear,
> Crouching in the remoteness of a fog-shrouded Sahara;

It is also not to be doubted that the thirteen-line central section of the poem, the richest in similes and metaphors, is the one that most obviously multiplies variations on the matrix image of the closed space of memory and death: "un gros meuble à tiroirs," "une pyramide, un immense caveau," "la fosse commune," "un cimetière," "un vieux boudoir . . . Où gît . . ." 'a big chest of drawers,' 'a pyramid, an immense burial vault,' 'potter's field,' 'a cemetery,' 'an old boudoir . . . Where lies . . .' The poem's meaning might be stated in this way: I am older, and more memory-laden, than death itself.

The weight of the death code (what a Barthes might have called the "*Mors* code") is such that it causes the momentary "death" of Mme Arnoux, permitting her to coalesce with the pathetic objects that metonymically evoke her and allowing Flaubert to exploit many elements of the descriptive system common to both texts. We may align a number of these in columnar display.

BAUDELAIRE	FLAUBERT
"souvenirs" 'memories/souvenirs'	"souvenirs" 'memories/souvenirs'
"Un gros meuble à tiroirs" 'a big chest of drawers'	"tous ses meubles!" 'all her furniture!'
"billets doux"[20] 'love letters'	"lettres d'amour" 'love letters'
"procès" 'lawsuit'	(the sale is the result of a *procès*)
"une pyramide, un immense caveau" 'a pyramid, an immense burial vault'	"l'Hôtel des commissaires-priseurs" 'the Auction Halls'
"morts," "fosse commune," "cimetière" 'the dead,' 'potter's field,' 'cemetery'	"une torpeur funèbre, une dissolution" 'a funeral torpor, a dissolution'
"de longs vers / Qui s'acharnent toujours sur mes morts les plus chers" 'long worms / Who always feed on my dearest dead'	"comme s'il avait vu des corbeaux déchiquetant son cadavre" 'as if he had seen crows tearing at her corpse'
"un vieux boudoir . . . / Où gît tout un fouillis de modes surannées" 'an old boudoir . . . / Where lies a heap of outmoded gowns'	"Ensuite, on vendit ses robes, puis un de ses chapeaux dont la plume cassée retombait, puis ses fourrures, puis trois paires de bottines" 'then her dresses were sold, then one of her hats with a drooping feather, then

20. Compare Rodolphe's perusal of the contents of his love-letter box: it includes "des bouquets, une jarretière, un masque noir, des épingles et des cheveux—des cheveux! de bruns, de blonds; quelques-uns même, s'accrochant à la ferrure de la boîte, se cassaient quand on l'ouvrait" 'bouquets, a garter, a black mask, pins and locks of hair—locks! brown ones, blond ones; and some of them, catching on the iron fittings, snapped when the box was opened.' Flaubert, *Madame Bovary*, 206. Baudelaire's poem contains "de lourds cheveux roulés dans des quittances" 'heavy locks rolled up in bills of receipt.'

her furs, then three pairs of her boots'

"l'odeur d'un flacon débouché" 'the odor of an unstoppered flask'

"Mme Dambreuse lui offrit son flacon" 'Mme Dambreuse offered him her flask'

"meuble à tiroirs," "pyramide," "caveau," "fosse," "cimetière," "boudoir" 'chest of drawers,' 'pyramid,' 'burial vault,' 'potter's field,' 'cemetery,' 'boudoir'

"coffret à fermoirs d'argent" 'box with silver clasps'

The foregoing confrontations show powerful semantic and lexical homologies and demonstrate the actualization of an antecedent, overdetermining descriptive system that contributes to the armature of monumentality in the auction of Mme Arnoux's belongings. There is mimesis in profusion, as is to be expected in a Realistic novel. There is multiple motivation, achieved through a sort of textual layering. Finally, and most convincingly to my mind, there is the resolution of catachresis, for the auction scene in nineteenth-century European literature is most evocative when it constitutes a *memento mori*.[21] Overdetermination entails the death of the goods' owner and explains why, throughout the scene, Frédéric acts as if Mme Arnoux were indeed dead. To dissuade Mme Dambreuse from bidding for the coffret, he begs her not to "dépouiller les morts de leurs secrets" 'strip the dead of their secrets.' The lady's tart rejoinder wrenches the text back to the mimetic level: "Je ne la croyais pas si morte" 'I didn't know she was as dead as all that.' Her comment could be considered an instance of embedded metalinguistic commentary to the extent that it draws attention to the artifices of the funereal code here catachretically activated to maintain an aesthetic effect: "the poetry of death."

From a verb, our language has made *memento* into a substantive, and thus into a concretization of memory. The coffret is the talismanic object of Frédéric's love for Mme Arnoux—not a

21. In a note Maynial cites Gabriele D'Annunzio's *Il Piacere* of 1889, in which the protagonist attends the public auction of his former mistress's furniture.

pure, unsullied Romantic love that would reach religious transcendence, like Amaury's for Mme de Couaën (for in Sainte-
Beuve's *Volupté* the lover-hero becomes a priest), but a love in the
post-Romantic vein of loss and *effritement*, a long erosion, the
slow, unremitting chipping and wasting away of the ideal, much
like Baudelaire's "granit entouré d'une vague épouvante" 'granite
surrounded by a nameless fear.' Flaubert's auctioneer tells the
potential bidders that with some polish ("blanc d'Espagne"—
the French term, by evoking Spain, is a marker of Romanticism) the coffret can gleam again. What price the monument
of love?

For a while it remains a bit tarnished, a little too dulled and
defiled in its passage from Mme Arnoux to Rosanette to Mme
Dambreuse. The coffret, our discomforting agent of time and
memory, lingers on as the site of a contingent signifier, as the
symbol of an enigmatic hollow: longing unfulfilled, potential
unrealized, the letter uninscribed.[22]

22. It is remarkable that Anthony, perhaps the most "Flaubertian" character of all,
should in all three versions of *La Tentation de Saint Antoine* be tempted by the Queen of
Sheba's ivory box, "un petit coffret chargé de ciselures." In each version she teases him
with her erotic secret: "Mais si tu savais ce que j'ai dans ma petite boîte! Retourne-la,
tâche de l'ouvrir! Personne n'y parviendra; embrasse-moi; je te le dirai. . . . Ah! ah! bel
ermite! tu ne le sauras pas! tu ne le sauras pas!" 'If you only knew what I've got in my
little box! Turn it over, try to open it! No one can succeed; kiss me; I'll tell you. . . . Oh!
oh! handsome hermit! You won't find out! You won't find out!' Flaubert, *Œuvres Complètes*, I, 434–35, 499, 532.

VIII ✺ History and Illusion in Flaubert's "Un Coeur simple"

The temptation to read Flaubert's "Un Coeur simple" as a statement on religion and even as the writer's profession of faith has proved irresistible to a generation of commentators. These readings range from Jean de La Varende's assertion that the tale shows a Flaubert ripe for conversion to the view that in it Flaubert satirizes and mocks religious institutions.[1] That Flaubert was consistently an unbeliever who consistently expressed reverence for the religious impulse (and indeed inscribed it at the very core of his thematics) does not deter such critics.[2] Flaubert's irony is detected in the proper names borne by the characters—Félicité, Théodore, Mme Aubain—and in the psittacism, or parrot fever, that presumably infects the universe of "Un

*This chapter is a revision of an article that appeared in the Winter, 1983, issue of the *Stanford French Review*, published by Anma Libri.

1. Jean de La Varende, *Flaubert par lui-même* (Paris, 1951), 154: Ben Stolzfus, "Point of View in 'Un Coeur simple,'" *French Review*, XXXV (1961), 19–25; Frederic J. Shepler, "La Mort et la rédemption dans les *Trois Contes* de Flaubert," *Neophilologus*, LXVI (1972), 407–16.

2. See Flaubert's letter to Mlle Leroyer de Chantepie: "And yet, what most attracts me is religion. I mean all religions, not one more than another. Each particular dogma repels me, but I consider the feeling that invented them as the most natural and most poetic of humanity." Gustave Flaubert, *Correspondance*, ed. Jean Bruneau (Paris, 1980), March 30, 1857.

Coeur simple." A typical summary of this position can be found in Michael Issacharoff, who writes that an ambiguous Loulou represents both "psittacism (for Flaubert) and the Holy Ghost (for Félicité): such a combination can only be satirical." Issacharoff, who takes an extreme position, asserts that Flaubert is a writer who mocks religion, and even states that the tale contains "an obvious anticlerical dimension."[3] Earlier, Enid Starkie, for her part, saw only pessimism in "Un Coeur simple." And Victor Brombert, while admitting irony, is the chief spokesman for the tale's "tenderness and compassion."[4]

A second group of critics might be termed the aesthetic school, or those who tend to view "Un Coeur simple" as an incipient *Kunstlerroman*. Robert Denommé, touching upon the growth in Félicité's creative imagination, attempts to refute ironic readings by pronouncing her a "child poet"; Harold Smith writes of a Loulou who has "the symbolic value of an attempt at esthetic creation similar to the work of the artist in Flaubert himself"; and Harry Cockerham seems to have summed up the position of those who see the tale as a parable of art when he writes, "Flaubert writes a tale marking the victory of art over reality."[5]

It is perhaps too much to make of Félicité a pre-Proustian celibate of art. I prefer to abandon religion and irony, concerns that are perhaps peculiar to Anglo-American literary culture, and take my cue from this observation by Albert Thibaudet: "The powers present at their deathbeds [Félicité's and Julien's] are powers of light, exactly the contrary of that power of darkness

3. Michael Issacharoff, *L'Espace et la nouvelle* (Paris, 1976), 35, 51. Ferdinand Brunetière seems to have inaugurated a long line of "ironic" critics; two of the best known are Luc Dariosecq and Paul A. Mankin. See Dariosecq, "A propos de Loulou," *French Review*, XXXI (1958), 22–24, and Mankin, "Additional Irony in 'Un Coeur simple,'" *French Review*, XXXV (1962), 411.

4. Enid Starkie, *Flaubert the Master* (New York, 1967), 260; Victor Brombert, *The Novels of Flaubert* (Princeton, 1966), 237.

5. Robert Denommé, "Félicité's View of Reality and the Nature of Flaubert's Irony in 'Un Coeur simple,'" *Studies in Short Fiction*, VII (1970), 573–81; Harold Smith, "Echec et illusion dans 'Un Coeur simple,'" *French Review*, XXXIX (October, 1965), 36–48; Harry Cockerham, "Sur la structure d''Un Coeur simple,'" *Travaux de Linguistique et de Littérature*, VIII (1970), 53–61.

that Flaubert, with the figure of the Blind Man, wished to place close to Emma Bovary as a symbol of her damnation, of her lost life. For the lives of Félicité and Julien, on the contrary, are victorious lives."[6]

In the first part of this chapter I shall examine how the historical shell of "Un Coeur simple"—its framing within the linear temporal flow of History—is shattered by the triumph of a fictive, imaginary world whose discourses supplant the "objective" ones of History and impose personal event—indeed illusion—as the gauge of truth value. Next I shall trace the development of one set of features of the inner discourse—the distributional, syntagmatic ordering of color and light in "Un Coeur simple." Finally, after examining this pattern, I shall pass to its affinitary, semantic relationship with the thematics of *Trois Contes* and of Flaubert's work as a whole. Although in my opinion the grand preoccupation of Flaubert's oeuvre is transcendence—sustenance through illusion—I have no doubt that this "thematic" statement is most difficult to establish and also that it is subject to constraints of a "writerly" nature. Thus, Barthes' remark concerning the primacy of the signifier in Flaubert remains a highly valid methodological signpost: "As is to be expected from a writer who continually absorbed content into form—or more precisely who contested that very antinomy—the linking of ideas is not experienced directly like a logical constraint, but must be defined in terms of the signifier.[7]

In two of the *Trois Contes*, Flaubert relies upon the reader's general cultural knowledge to provide the historical context of the fiction: the time of Christ for "Hérodias," the Middle Ages for "Saint Julien." The tale's time span may be either short (the former) or long (the latter) without producing much effect on the reader, for beyond these vague historical settings, not much more information is either required or expected. If we turn to longer "historical" fictions—such as *Salammbô*—we find that this is also true. However, with the possible exception of *Ma-*

6. Albert Thibaudet, *Gustave Flaubert* (Paris, 1935), 194.
7. Roland Barthes, "Flaubert et la phrase," *Word*, XXIV (1968), 52.

dame Bovary, this is not valid for works with contemporary (*i.e.*, nineteenth-century) settings. History undergirds and structures *L'Education sentimentale* (and to a lesser degree, *Bouvard et Pécuchet*), and numerous chronological references frame its development, from the opening sentence of "The 15th of September, 1840 . . ." to the penultimate chapter's "Toward the end of March, 1867 . . ." Grand events (Frédéric's personal "reform" of 1848 and the coup d'état of 1851, which coincides with Frédéric's sentimental defeat) move in tandem with individual destiny, so that we can say that history matches History.

With its contemporary setting, "Un Coeur simple" might be expected to exhibit a similar homology between the fortunes of French society and the tribulations of individual destiny, and at first glance there is indeed a large number of historical dates relative to the number of pages in the tale. These precise dates are mentioned: 1809, 1819, 1825, 1827, 1828, "the July Revolution," 1837, 1853. In addition, there is a reference to the horrors of 1793 and to Polish refugees of the 1830 anti-Russian uprising. Thus, a familiar writing style, the discourse of history, seems to attach Flaubert's tale to nineteenth-century chronology and to ensnare fictional event in the web of History. Dates in such profusion constitute apparent indices of successivity in "Un Coeur simple." The "outer" event—the *hors texte*—would thus stand as a sociological imperative of sorts, enclosing Féli cité within a positivistic system in which her progress would be fundamentally linear and causal (and perhaps metonymical)—a temporal slide into the senility of parrot worship and death. It is clear, however, that the system of temporal references in "Un Coeur simple" actually subverts this relationship of the collective and the individual. More precisely, it *inverts* it. Far from a relationship of *Histoire* to *histoire* (literary "realism"), that of History enclosing a story—a History under erasure—we discover a History that is dissolved by individual event, itself relegated to the ash can of insignificance. And in place of the linear, Flaubert will substitute the cyclical; for the causal, the associative or the coincidental; and for the metonymical chain of dissimilar events, the metaphorical resemblance of sameness.

We might say that in "Un Coeur simple," History is shunted aside, left "unanalyzed."

With precise historical dates, as is the case with all of the years cited above, Flaubert's practice is twofold. Either he picks dates with no particular historical significance (and thus without possibility of semantic resonance with fictional event), or conversely, he invests the historically insignificant with personal significance: "Thus, in 1825, two glaziers whitewashed the vestibule; in 1827, a portion of the roof falling into the courtyard nearly killed a man. In the summer of 1828, it was Madame's turn to distribute the consecrated bread."[8] He also demythologizes grand historical years. There is only one such date in the tale—1830—and the mechanism of its dehistoricization is easily grasped. "One night, the coach driver announced the July Revolution in Pont-l'Evêque. A new subprefect, a few days later, was appointed: the Baron de Larsonnière, a former consul in America" (47).

No one in Pont-l'Evêque is touched enough by History to lament the departure of the Bourbons or applaud the advent of freedom of the press. The *Charte*, Louis-Philippe, the *tricolore*—all are unmentioned, for the Revolution of 1830 is experienced in purely personal terms: a new family, with ties to the exotic New World (as "other" worldly as the *géographie en estampes* is for Félicité), comes to town. This family's most distinctive features are their Negro servant and their parrot; thus, at the end of the chapter, with Loulou's entry into Madame Aubain's household, the text imparts the following information in a completing analepsis: "For a long time he had occupied Félicité's imagination, for he came from America, and this word reminded her of Victor, so that she asked the Negro about him. Once she had even said: 'Wouldn't Madame love to have him!'" (51).

And as if to deny explicitly the lay, political significance of 1830, the text actually proposes a mystical origin for the parrot, making him, through lack of logical transition, into a divine re-

8. Gustave Flaubert, *Trois Contes*, ed. E. Maynial (Paris, 1961), 46–47. All page references in the text are to this edition.

compense for the care Félicité has lavished upon Père Colmiche: "He [Père Colmiche] died; she had a mass said for the repose of his soul. That day a great happiness came to her" (50–51). The great happiness was the gift of Loulou.

Thus "1830," while enjoying great thematic importance, joins 1825, 1827, 1828, etc., as a date without external referent, without reverberation in History. In addition, Père Colmiche and 1830 are semantically associated through the concept of revolution—for the old man was allegedly guilty of crimes during the Terror: "he was said to have committed horrors in '93." The relationship between Loulou, on one hand, and Père Colmiche and the July Revolution, on the other, is not historical or ideological, or even symbolical (if we could imagine the highly visual Félicité contemplating and responding to revolutionary iconology, such as Delacroix's *La Liberté sur les barricades*). Rather that relationship is theological and, especially, *metaphorical:* they possess the common seme of exotic love.

I have said that 1830 was the only potentially "external" date in "Un Coeur simple," but there is actually a second "revolutionary" date lying at the intersection, as it were, of the personal and the historical. This is the date on which Victor announces that he has signed on for a long-term voyage. Interestingly, it is the day of the announcement (Monday) rather than that of his actual departure (two days later, on Wednesday) that stands out in Félicité's memory, in the same way that prophecy or cultural event eclipses accomplishment: "Un lundi, 14 juillet 1819 (elle n'oublia pas la date), Victor annonça qu'il était engagé au long cours, et, dans la nuit du surlendemain, par le paquebot de Honfleur, irait rejoindre sa goélette, qui devait démarrer du Havre prochainement" (32) 'One Monday, July 14, 1819 (she did not forget the date), Victor announced that he had signed on for a long voyage, and, two nights later, would take the Honfleur packet, to join up with his schooner, which was to weigh anchor at Le Havre very soon.'

Although one could pause to reflect upon the syntactical-psychological precipitates of this single sentence, especially those accumulating after the conjunction *et* (highlighted by its two commas), two features are of particular chronological relevance here. The first is the apparent foregrounding of yet another date of historical significance, this time the evocation of July 14, the *fête nationale*, the Grand Revolution. But what it might contain of historical import is immediately thwarted or neutralized by the insignificance of the year—1819.

The second feature is of course the unusually affirmative, thus obtrusive mark of the narrating agent that comes in the parentheses ("elle n'oublia pas la date"). Its effect is to redirect this freshly destroyed (self-canceling) historical date toward history, the *événement intérieur*, and away from History. The specificity of the date lies in its coincidence not with the Revolution, but with the revolution of individual destiny. This is history, we might say, of the *Annales* school.

In contrast with the blurred intrusions of History, the date-marking events of Félicité's microhistory are experienced and recounted with a striking precision and wealth of chronological detail. A typical example is the family's trip to Trouville for the sea baths. Preparations begin "the night before," with the sending off of the main baggage. "The next day" the trip begins; the road is in such poor condition that it requires "two hours" to cover the eight kilometers between Pont-l'Evêque and Madame Aubain's farm in Toucques. In the course of the journey there are numerous allusions to the past: to Théodore, to grandparents, to the manifest aging of the tenants and their establishment. After a copious meal, it requires "another half hour" to reach Trouville; finally, "three minutes later," the inn courtyard is reached.

Another typical sequence also involves Virginie's failing health. Madame has arranged to visit her daughter "every Tuesday," and all appears settled. "Autumn slipped gently by." Then comes an interruption: "But one evening . . ." This is the news of Virginie's attack, and with it comes a flurry of temporal indicators marking Virginie's sudden illness, death, and burial. In the space of three pages (42–44), the precipitous rush of the sequence is carefully plotted.

Night was about to fall. . . . Then she ran after the gig and caught up with it an hour later. . . . The next day, right at dawn, she went to the doctor's. . . . Finally, at twilight, she took the Lisieux coach. . . . Félicité banged the knocker hard. . . . After a few minutes. . . . The good sister . . . told her that "she had just passed away." At that moment, the bell of Saint-Léonard rang harder than ever. . . . For two nights, Félicité did not leave the dead girl. . . . At the end of the first vigil. . . . After the mass, it took another three-quarters of an hour to reach the cemetery.[9]

What establishes the punctuality, the sharpness, of these episodes is the manner in which they interrupt routine, the established temporal rhythms that regulate Félicité's life. These routines are personal and religious. They involve social habits such as Madame Aubain's regular ("on Thursdays . . .") card-party guests ("They arrived promptly at eight and withdrew before the stroke of eleven") and Victor's regular visits to Félicité ("He came on Sundays, after Mass. . . . At the first knell of Vespers, she would wake him"). They also involve routines of domestic economy, in which we see Félicité collecting her mistress's rents ("Every Monday morning, about noon . . .") or accomplishing ritual, immemorial household gestures ("Félicité turned her spinning wheel in the kitchen"). The routinized is, however, never seen being established. Somehow it is always already there, presupposing, as it were, the very repetition that marks it as such—as habitual. Its origin is never glimpsed, but only affirmed by the repetitious imperfect tense. Properly speaking, it cannot be *traced*, only localized in the vague yet broad temporal ellipses of the beginning that is the tale's given: "For a half century . . ."

Even startled moments can be absorbed by routine, as shown in the unusual terminal imperfect tense of "Le curé discourait, les enfants récitaient, elle finissait par s'endormir; et *se réveillait tout à coup*" (27; italics added) 'The priest would preach, the children would recite, she would drop off; and *would awaken all at once.*"

If routine interrupted by dramatic event (usually death, as we

9. A third personal event heavily marked by precise temporal references is Félicité's brief love affair with Théodore (9–11).

have seen in the case of Victor and Virginie—a type of temporal elasticizing through a profusion of chronological notations) is one means of marking the passage of time in "Un Coeur simple," there are at least two other schemes worthy of note. There is the *annulling* of time, in which events of great personal import seem to follow hard upon one another; the events may be in fact separated by a temporal lapse of some duration, but psychologically they touch. In this way, Virginie's death seems to come immediately after Victor's. The technique Flaubert uses to effect this leap is to "erase" time, by inserting after the letter announcing Victor's death a proleptic narration of the circumstances of that death: "Much later, from Victor's captain himself, she learned the circumstances of his end." After this, apart from the allusion to a lack of communication between Félicité and Victor's parents, the text passes virtually without temporal transition to the narration of Virginie's fatal illness. The coincidence of the two deaths makes Félicité's feeling of a double death at Virginie's burial all the more plausible: "Elle songeait à son neveu, et n'ayant pu lui rendre ces honneurs, avait un surcroît de tristesse, comme si on l'eût enterré avec l'autre" (44) 'She thought of her nephew, and not having been able to do him these honors, experienced an added grief, just as if he were being buried with her.'

A second example of temporal eclipse comes between Madame Aubain's death (and the heirs' decision to put the house up for sale) and the final six pages on Félicité's own agony and death. The transitional phrase is strongly marked by reflexive structures: "Des années se passèrent. Et la maison ne se louait pas, et ne se vendait pas" (67) 'Many years passed. And the house failed to rent or to sell.'

If, following Proust, we admire the "blank spaces" of *L'Education sentimentale*'s ending, we might recall that there Flaubert had simply written, "Des années passèrent." In "Un Coeur simple" years pass all by themselves, unaided, triply marked by the emptiness of nonevent and doubly marked by what I shall call Flaubert's disjunctive conjunction, *et*—concerning which

Proust again was the first to teach that "it marks a pause in a rhythmical measure and divides a tableau."[10]

The superimposition of deaths (Virginie and Victor, Madame Aubain and Félicité) suggests the third chronological pattern in "Un Coeur simple"—*cyclical time*. In examining what he calls a "rhetoric of repetition" in *Trois Contes*, Marc Bertrand writes that "this iterative structure's function is to attenuate the importance of historical time in favor of the time of the narration . . . the time of the inner story of the central character."[11] It is in fact the Church calendar that constitutes the "real" time of the story: Pâques, la Fête-Dieu, l'Assomption, la Toussaint, Noël—the repetition of religious feasts that seems so natural to Félicité and that abolishes time as successivity and change, establishing in their place return and re-cognition. Thus, the biblical and the mythical function as representations of the timeless: "Les semailles, les moissons, les pressoirs, toutes ces choses familières dont parle l'Evangile, se trouvaient dans sa vie; le passage de Dieu les avait sanctifiées; et elle aima plus tendrement les agneaux par amour de l'Agneau, les colombes à cause du Saint-Esprit" (26) 'The sowing of the seed, the reaping of the harvest, the pressing of the grapes, all these familiar things the Scriptures speak of, were to be found in her life; God in passing had sanctified them; and she loved the lambs more tenderly for love of the Lamb, and the doves for the sake of the Holy Ghost.'

This sentence erases chronological flow by rendering coeval scriptural time and Félicité's time. History is occulted: only pastoral essences, unchanging fixities, persist. Thus, in this world of permanence, change can be considered only as a variation of the same, and never as difference. Since history for Félicité is a process of paradigmatic or metaphorical substitutions (the lamb for the Lamb), there is no impediment to the substitution of parrot for dove. Moreover, the paradigmatic nature of existence

10. Marcel Proust, "A propos du 'style' de Flaubert," in Proust, *Contre Sainte-Beuve*, ed. Pierre Clarac (Paris, 1971), 595, 591.
11. Marc Bertrand, "Parole et silence dans les *Trois Contes* de Flaubert," *Stanford French Review*, I (1977), 193.

allows for a high degree of psychological identification, a process favored by Félicité's great capacity for love. At Virginie's first communion Félicité, "with the imagination that true affection gives," nearly *becomes* the young girl. During Victor's sea voyage Félicité *feels for* her nephew: on sunny days she thirsts, and during storms she fears the lightning. And when Félicité understands that her final illness has been diagnosed as pneumonia, she softly murmurs, "'Ah! comme madame,' trouvant naturel de suivre sa maîtresse" "'Ah! like Madame," finding it natural to follow her mistress.' Félicité is endowed with what might be called the gift of unitary existence, in which space as well as time is not so much abolished as collocated—experienced as a sameness.

In keeping with its cyclical structure, the first sentence of "Un Coeur simple" can now be seen to set its tone: "Pendant un demi-siècle, les bourgeoises de Pont-l'Evêque envièrent à Madame Aubain sa servante Félicité" 'For a half century, the women of Pont-l'Evêque envied Madame Aubain her servant Félicité.' *Un demi-siècle* clearly is psychologically longer—much longer—than "fifty years" would be, and we even have some documentary evidence in Flaubert's other writings for this assertion. In *Madame Bovary*, Félicité's double, one Catherine-Nicaise-Elisabeth Leroux, is awarded a gold medal for "fifty-four years of service on the same farm," and the narrator satirizes bourgeois smugness by stating: "Ainsi se tenait devant ces bourgeois épanouis ce demi-siècle de servitude" 'Thus before these beaming bourgeois stood this half century of servitude.' Thus, inner time outweighs (in density) measured linear time from the very beginning of "Un Coeur simple," and the first references to Félicité frame her in a cyclical existence: "Elle se levait dès l'aube, pour ne pas manquer la messe, et travaillait jusqu'au soir sans interruption; puis, le dîner étant fini, la vaisselle en ordre et la porte bien close, elle enfouissait la bûche sous les cendres et s'endormait devant l'âtre, son rosaire à la main" 'She would arise at dawn so as not to miss mass, and work till evening without stopping; then, the dinner over, the dishes put away and the door bolted, she would bury the log under the ashes and fall asleep in front of the hearth, her rosary in her hands.'

In one syntactical unit, the sentence takes us, "without stopping," from sunup to sundown and establishes Félicité as the guardian of hearth and home, faithful to routines both domestic and religious, leading an existence marked by the metaphorical repetitiveness of the rosary in her hand. Her costume is unchanging ("All year round she wore a calico kerchief fastened behind with a pin"), her age indeterminate ("After age fifty, she no longer seemed to be of any age"). Félicité's life does not constitute an itinerary so much as it does an iteration.

In composing *L'Education sentimentale*, Flaubert had expressed the fear that his characters might be "dévorés par les fonds historiques" 'devoured by the historical background.' The relationship of history and History in "Un Coeur simple" is entirely different. Indeed, here it is History that yields to the *événement intérieur*, for it becomes an "outer" presence, a mere foil to the arresting triumph of metaphorical time. In "Un Coeur simple," Flaubert valorizes, mythologizes history with a small *h*—or the imaginary, the realm of fiction itself.[12] Thus, the triumph of the trivial. "Des événements intérieurs faisaient une date, où l'on se reportait plus tard" 'Private events marked dates that they later referred to.'

To return briefly to the famous opening sentence of "Un Coeur simple," we can see that it apparently sets Mme Aubain over and against Félicité. Semantically it establishes Mme Aubain's social ascendancy; yet syntactically, if we disregard the bourgeois degrees of "Madame" and "servant," it merely *juxtaposes* two women, two characters. It is as if the phrasing attempted simultaneously to present a combination both arbitrary and yet hierarchical. We have noted the psychological length of "half

12. The objective pretensions of historical writing—and the parallels with fiction writing, particularly during the French Realistic period—are characterized as "referential illusions" in one of Barthes' most subtle essays: "Le Discours de l'histoire," *Poétique*, XLIX (1982), 13–21.

century" and have seen in invoking a parallel context in *Madame Bovary* that its latent signified, or matrix, is servitude. In the end, however, the phrase focuses entirely upon Félicité as the object of the tale, Félicité, whose name stands as a kind of vanishing point for the little historical tableau brushed in one rich line.

The line suggests a series of parallels that could be traced throughout the story, but I shall focus on color and light, as manifested in vision in particular, as one that is most revealing to follow. Moreover, it can aid in situating the tale's celebrated closing line, with its alleged irony: "elle crut voir, dans les cieux entrouverts, un perroquet gigantesque, planant au-dessus de sa tête" 'she thought she saw, in the opening heavens, a gigantic parrot hovering above her head.' This parallel—really an opposition—will center on Félicité's much examined final vision and the little-mentioned "manifestation" (in the sense this word would have in a séance) recounted by Mme Aubain.

Félicité is from the beginning associated with light, color, and vision, whereas the description of Mme Aubain's house, with its emphasis on loss and faded pretension, contains few mentions of color. Those that are presented stress a decolorized or monochromatic interior: white wall panelings, the pallid flowers of the wallpaper, a black wooden desk, pen-and-ink drawings, watery gouaches—all, in the narrator's terms, "memories of a better time and a vanished luxury." The sentence immediately following sets the servant's world in subtle but sharp contrast with the lightless quarters of her mistress: "Une lucarne au second étage éclairait la chambre de Félicité, ayant vue sur les prairies" 'On the third floor a dormer window gave light to Félicité's room, with its view of the fields.' Light is thrice underscored ("lucarne," "éclairait," "vue"), and the last term in the series, *les prairies*, emphasizes access to the pastoral world whose openness stands in opposition to Mme Aubain's drawing room, which was always shut up. Moreover, the connotations of "prairie," contrasted with the mold of Mme Aubain's dwelling—for the whole apartment smells "a bit musty"—suggest a relation of fertility to infertility and indeed of a biblical world of Life and revelation in opposition to the tomblike apartment below, where the floor is "below the level of the garden."

Félicité's world is first of all, at the Colleville fair, one of dazzle, of *éblouissement:* "Tout de suite elle fut étourdie, stupéfaite par le tapage des ménétriers, les lumières dans les arbres, la bigarrure des costumes, les dentelles, les croix d'or, cette masse de monde sautant à la fois" 'She was immediately dazzled, stupefied by the noise of the fiddlers, the lights in the trees, the gaily colored costumes, the lace, the gold crosses, the throng of people gigging all together.' Here visual elements predominate, and *lumières* and *bigarrure* are proleptic features intimating the appearance of Loulou, the brightly colored bird of paradise: "Son front corps était *vert,* le bout de ses ailes *rose,* son front *bleu,* et sa gorge *dorée*" (italics added) 'His body was *green,* the tips of his wings *pink,* his crown *blue,* and his breast *golden.*' The bonds between Félicité and Loulou are thus chromaticized.[13] The fair scene is in essence replicated in the explosively variegated scene at the end in which cascades of flowers inundate the altar of repose. There we find a new *dentelle,* a *soleil d'or* (touches of gold are never absent, and range from the name of the inn, "L'Agneau d'or" 'The Golden Lamb,' and the gilded nut the stuffed Loulou cockily grasps in his beak, to phonetic name plays such as Théodore and Victor), and of course the *vapeur d'azur* that fills Félicité with mystical sensuality.

The passage from Colleville to Corpus Christi is yet another aspect of Félicité's path from profane to sacred, from materiality to illusion. That this should be accomplished *psychologically* through the parrot is a result of the well-known confusion in her mind between the parrot and the Holy Ghost as depicted in the church window. In the stained glass the essence of the tale is shown, for there a virgin is "dominated" by the Holy Ghost. But more important, the symbolic dove is modified in her mind

---

13. In one of the *carnets* of "Un Coeur simple," a protodescription of the "costume de pont-L'Evêque" emphasized color: "Robe violette, chapeau jaune . . . gants verts . . . des robes rouges" 'Scarlet dress, yellow hat . . . green gloves . . . red dresses.' George Willenbrink, *The Dossier of Flaubert's "Un Coeur simple"* (Amsterdam, 1976), 99.

to a parrot. The realization of this metamorphosis, Félicité's own consciousness of it, comes only after Loulou's demise, specifically in a reference that makes the link in a visual manner: "A l'eglise, elle contemplait toujours le Saint-Esprit, et observa qu'il avait quelque chose du perroquet. Sa ressemblance lui parut encore plus manifeste sur une image d'Epinal.[14]. . . . Avec ses ailes de *pourpre* et son corps d'*émeraude*, c'était vraiment le portrait de Loulou" (62–63; italics added) 'In church she always contemplated the Holy Ghost, and noticed that he looked something like the parrot. His similarity appeared even more obvious on an Epinal print. . . . With his wings of *purple* and his *emerald* body, he was truly the picture of Loulou.'

The ennobling vocabulary (*rose* > *pourpre; vert* > *émeraude*) is the first lexical step in a paradoxical process whereby Flaubert lends substance to illusion. I shall return to this point. In the meantime, let us label this process *accretive;* it is a paradigmatic thickening or metaphoric layering and substitution. In its accumulation it corresponds to the enrichment characterizing Félicité's existence: assimilation, not dissipation; assumption, not abjection.

Another aspect of this assimilation can be perceived in the appropriation and naturalization of the biblical in Félicité's microcosm. This is realized through an imaginative integration of twin pastoral and agricultural societies, a gemination that permits the concordance of sacred and profane: as we have seen, her love for the Lamb of God enriches her love of lambs, and she loves the dove for the sake of the Holy Ghost. Thus, the church's wood carving depicting Saint Michael conquering the dragon might be transformed visually into an equivalent "Saint Félicité conquering the bull." According to Flaubert's original scenario, Félicité was also to have a mysterious sway over beasts: her "great gentleness" was to be accompanied by a "magnetic power over animals, chickens, bees, dogs, however wild."[15]

14. Another "document" in Félicité's existence is the illustrated geography book, which originally was a "géographie en images coloriées" 'geography book with *colored* images' (italics added). See Willenbrink, *The Dossier of Flaubert's "Un Coeur simple,"* 83.

15. Willenbrink, *The Dossier of Flaubert's "Un Coeur simple,"* 82, 137. Raymonde Debray-Genette points out that Flaubert eventually deleted this "Fioretti side" of her

Félicité's assimilation comes to her through the catechism and through the priest's telescoped presentation of religious history, which provokes an *éblouissement* in Mme Aubain's maidservant.[16] When it comes to the Holy Ghost, Félicité imagines this abstraction as a fire or as a light flying in the clouds: "Il n'était pas seulement oiseau, mais encore un feu, et d'autres fois un souffle. C'est peut-être sa lumière qui voltige la nuit au bord des marécages, son haleine qui pousse les nuées" 'he was not only a bird, but a fire as well, and at other times a breath. It was perhaps his light that flits about the edge of the marshes at night, his breath driving the clouds.'

The clustered images of light and afflation in this passage are psychologically and metaphorically equivalent to the loud colors of the last scene, the breath and clouds to its incense (and through the cigar smoke to far-off Havana, to Victor and the exotic land of Loulou's origin). The verb *voltiger* 'to flit' is used once more in the tale in connection with Loulou and color: when Loulou is feared lost, Félicité frantically searches for him throughout Pont-l'Evêque, seeing—or rather *believing* she sees—"une chose verte qui voltigeait" 'a green thing flitting.'[17] All this is compressed in the final paragraph into the image of the azure cloud and the gigantic parrot.

Loulou, like Théodore and all the other objects of Félicité's affection, is truly a divine gift. As we have seen, he comes to her, almost as a recompense, on the day of Père Colmiche's death. The parrot's relationship with Félicité, the narrator tells

---

existence. See Debray-Genette, "La Technique romanesque de Flaubert dans 'Un Coeur simple,'" in Michael Issacharoff (ed.), *Langages de Flaubert* (Paris, 1976), 95–107. Earlier, D. L. Demorest had noted this "instinctual identification" between Félicité's life and the Bible in his *L'Expression figurée et symbolique dans l'oeuvre de Gustave Flaubert* (Geneva, 1967), 581.

16. It is interesting to compare the effectiveness of this priest's catechism and the failed lesson of l'abbé Bournisien in *Madame Bovary:* there the children's droning repetition ("étant baptisé, baptisé, baptisé") has been called the parroting of inefficient grace. See Brombert, *The Novels of Flaubert,* 70–71.

17. A dictionary synonym of *voltiger* being *papillonner* (see *Petit Robert*), we can perhaps perceive in the butterflies of Virginie's wardrobe ("des papillons s'envolèrent de l'armoire" 'butterflies flew out of the wardrobe') another image of redemption—through the association in Christian symbology of Psyche, the soul, and the resurrection.

us, is virtually that of son or lover, and the union is made explicit in a typically Flaubertian phrase that joins the human to the animal: "les grandes ailes du bonnet et les ailes de l'oiseau frémissaient ensemble" 'the big plumes of the hat and the bird's wings trembled in unison.' The harmony of this love relationship is the obverse of the hate relationship, filled with mutual loathing, that had marked Julien's rapport with the animal world. ("La Légende de Saint Julien" was the first composed of the *Trois Contes;* the disturbing relation between man and animal is an early preoccupation of Flaubert, as evidenced in *Quidquid volueris* and the man-ape Djalioh.) It is strikingly reminiscent, especially in its contrast, of the scene that leads Julien to abandon home and parents in order to avoid fulfilling the terrible prophecy of parricide made by the great stag. In that scene Julien hurls his javelin at what he thinks is a stork, but he has actually taken aim at the feathers of his mother's coif. The contrast between the two episodes points to the differences in the respective characters. Julien can only achieve sainthood by setting himself against nature, and in undergoing terrible sufferings and deprivations, before attaining salvation in kissing the leper, an act of total self-abnegation. Yet, Félicité—"pour de pareilles âmes le surnaturel est tout simple" 'for such souls the supernatural is entirely simple'—effortlessly reaches a pantheistic union with the natural world.[18] Julien's religion is a tortuous way of the cross, with stations ranging from the beggar's bowl to the imperial palace; Félicité's is a simple, Franciscan humility and a steady acceptance of mortification.

What is more, Félicité's visions have a genuineness that is most convincing when compared with those of Mme Aubain. At first glance, there seems hardly to be any correspondence in

18. See also the passage in *Voyage en Italie et en Suisse* in which Flaubert recounts a dream in which he and his mother are surrounded in a forest by monkeys. When one of them takes his hand, Flaubert shoots the animal, thus incurring his mother's reproach: "'Why are you wounding your friend? what did he do to you? can't you see that he loves you? how much like you he looks!' . . . This wrenched my soul and I awakened . . . feeling a natural bond to the animals and fraternizing with them *in a tender, pantheistic union*" (italics added). Gustave Flaubert, *Œuvres Complètes*, Collection L'Integrale (2 vols.; Paris, 1964), II, 460.

kind or quality. Corresponding to the mistress's love for her daughter, there is Félicité's for her nephew. To the somewhat intimidating memory of "Monsieur," so assiduously cultivated by Mme Aubain, corresponds the parrot. The relationship between these objects of love seems to be one of nonrecognition, distance, and psychological disjuncture when framed in a brief and again typically Flaubertian exchange between mistress and servant. As Mme Aubain frets for lack of news or letters from Virginie, Félicité thinks to console her by saying:

"Moi, madame, voilà six mois que je n'en ai reçu! . . ."
"De qui donc? . . ."
La servante répliqua doucement:
"Mais . . . de mon neveu!"
"Ah! votre neveu!" Et, haussant les épaules, Mme Aubain reprit sa promenade, ce qui voulait dire, "Je n'y pensais pas! . . . Au surplus, je m'en moque! un mousse, un gueux, belle affaire! . . . tandis que ma fille . . . Songez donc! . . ."
Félicité, bien que nourrie dans la rudesse, fut indignée contre Madame, puis oublia.

"Madame, I've been six months without news! . . ."
"News of whom? . . ."
The servant softly answered·
"Why . . . of my nephew!"
"Oh! your nephew!" And shrugging her shoulders, she continued her walk, which was to say, "I wasn't thinking of him! . . . Besides, I don't care about him! a cabin boy, a wretch, that's all! . . . Whereas my daughter . . . Just think! . . ."
Even with her harsh upbringing, Félicité was indignant with Madame, then forgot.

In *Salammbô* the same gulf separates Hamilcar and the slave father whose son the Suffete proposes to sacrifice in place of his own (Hannibal) during the sanguinary rites of placation of Moloch. The father timidly asks, "Est-ce que tu vas le . . . ?" 'Are you going to . . .?' not daring to finish his question, and Hamilcar looks at him in astonishment.

Il n'avait jamais pensé,—tant l'abîme les séparant l'un de l'autre se trouvait immense,—qu'il pût y avoir entre eux rien de commun. Cela même lui parut une sorte d'outrage et d'empiètement sur ses privilèges.

Il répondit par un regard plus froid et plus lourd que la hache d'un bourreau; l'esclave s'évanouissant tomba dans la poussière, à ses pieds. Hamilcar enjamba par-dessus.[19]

He had never considered—so immense was the abyss separating the two—that there could be anything in common between them. Even this seemed like a sort of outrage and infringement of his privileges. He answered with a look that was colder and heavier than an executioner's ax; fainting, the slave fell into the dust at his feet. Hamilcar stepped over him.

The socially and psychologically unbridgeable gap, however, is closed in "Un Coeur simple," and even reversed in the all-important death scene, if we compare it with the curious and little-remarked scene where Mme Aubain tells Félicité of an obsessive dream and of an apparition. Here there are links and contrasts with the twin cults (that is, "Monsieur" and Virginie versus Victor and Loulou). In the dream "Monsieur" appears in sailor's garb and is just returning from a long voyage, which relates him to Victor, the sailor boy, and his passage to Havana. This link is closely followed by other prefigurative ones, for the description of Virginie's tomb, with its column of pink marble surrounded by beds of flowers, is the forerunner of the still more glittering altar of repose that enshrines Loulou in the final chapter. Félicité, ever combining the symbolic or scriptural with the literal, matches her mistress's cult of the dead by genuflecting in a physical act of cultivation: she kneels to weed, to water, to replenish the sand around the grave. And in the apparition, Virginie and "Monsieur" appear to Mme Aubain one day in the garden: "Une fois, elle rentra du jardin, bouleversée. Tout à l'heure (elle montrait l'endroit) le père et la fille lui étaient apparus l'un auprès de l'autre, et ils ne faisaient rien; ils la regardaient. Pendant plusieurs mois, elle resta dans sa chambre, inerte" (45) 'One day she came in from the garden completely upset. Just then (she pointed to the spot) the father and the daughter had appeared to her standing side by side, doing nothing; they were looking at her. For several months she stayed in her room, immobilized.'

19. Gustave Flaubert, *Salammbô*, in *Œuvres Complètes*, I, 778.

The flatness or neutrality of the narrative voice in this passage is suspect, for it is the same as the damning objectivity with which Swedenborg's spiritual peregrinations are presented in the passage of *Bouvard et Pécuchet* devoted to *spiritisme:* "Swedenborg a fait de grands voyages [dans les espaces lumineux]. Car, en moins d'un an, il a exploré Vénus, Mars, Saturne, et vingt-trois fois Jupiter. De plus, il a vu à Londres Jésus-Christ, il a vu Saint-Paul, il a vu Saint-Jean, il a vu Moïse, et, en 1736, il a même vu le jugement dernier"[20] 'Swedenborg made long trips [in the luminous spaces]. For in less than a year, he explored Venus, Mars, Saturn, and, twenty-three times, Jupiter. Moreover, in London he saw Jesus Christ, he saw Saint Paul, he saw Saint John, he saw Moses, and, in 1736, he even saw the Last Judgment.' The circumstantially precise details, "in 1736" and "she pointed to the spot," and the unruffled calmness of the assertions merely serve to heighten the reader's skepticism and also to induce a certain amount of bafflement. How ironical it is, in the case of Flaubert, that his readers should have become accustomed to finding that *some* narrational signal is less disturbing than none at all! And since Flaubert's interventions are often indications of sympathy, their absence inclines one to conclude for a tongue-in-cheek authorial attitude.

To continue with the apparition before Mme Aubain, it is worth noting another revealing absence in this episode, that of verbs of seeming, verbs that precisely *seem* to attenuate the credibility of vision while the context confirms its authenticity, thus converting them into verbs of credence. The important combination *croire* and *voir* occurs three times in "Un Coeur simple." The first associates the combination with the sacred and with vision, the second with Loulou, and the third with redemption (the italics have been added).

1. Le prêtre fit d'abord un abrégé de l'Histoire Sainte. Elle *croyait voir* le paradis, le déluge, la tour de Babel, des villes tout en flammes, des peuples qui mouraient, des idoles renversées; et elle garda de cet *éblouissement* le respect du Trés-Haut et de sa colère. (25–26)

20. Gustave Flaubert, *Bouvard et Pécuchet*, in *Œuvres Complètes*, II, 267.

First, the priest gave a short outline of sacred history. She *thought she could see* the Garden of Eden, the Flood, the Tower of Babel, towns aflame, peoples dying, idols overthrown; and of this *dazzling vision* she retained respect for the Almighty and His wrath.

2. Tout à coup elle *crut distinguer* derrière les moulins, au bas de la côte, une chose verte qui voltigeait. (55)

All of a sudden she *thought she could see*, behind the mills, at the bottom of the hill, a green thing flying.

3. Et, quand elle exhala son dernier souffle, elle *crut voir*, dans les cieux entrouverts, un perroquet gigantesque, planant au-dessus de sa tête. (73)

And, as she breathed her last, she *thought she could see*, in the opening heavens, a gigantic parrot, hovering above her head.

For most commentators, *crut voir* reveals irony, though A. W. Raitt says it expresses sadness. For Ben Stolzfus "Un Coeur simple" is a "strong attack on religion," and the *crut voir* of the end "obliquely injects Flaubert's final negation of her most cherished vision. This negation creates the void, the very absence of comfort which her religion is expected to provide. She did not see, she only *thought* she saw. This is Flaubert's concluding statement." More cautiously and more advisedly, George Willenbrink notes that on draft page 340v of "Un Coeur simple," Flaubert had written, "Elle voyait le Saint-Esprit perroquet au-dessus de sa tête souriante" 'She saw the Holy Ghost parrot above her smiling head.' For him, this is less assertive than "elle vit" would have been, and thus *crut voir* is a compromise of sorts: Flaubert does not wish either to endorse or to fully "deny the vision outright." T. A. Unwin notes that it is the narrator, not Félicité, who shows awareness of the parrot's decay: the character thus remains enveloped in illusion.[21]

But the *crut voir* serves not to invalidate or deflate some illusory, unsubstantial belief; it would be the very *absence* of such combinations that would problematize the objective status of "fact," in the way that absence operates in *Bouvard et Pécuchet*.

21. A. W. Raitt, "Un Coeur simple," in Peter Nurse (ed.), *The Art of Criticism* (Edinburgh, 1969), 213; Stolzfus, "Point of View in 'Un Coeur simple,'" 24; Willenbrink, *The Dossier of Flaubert's "Un Coeur simple*," 229; T. A. Unwin, "La Présence de Flaubert dans les *Trois Contes*," *Les Amis de Flaubert*, LIII (December, 1978), 12–20.

Far from being a signal of skepticism, *crut voir* is one of affirmation, for it asserts the sustaining powers of illusion. Here one recalls a Flaubertian project entitled "La Spirale," which was published in 1958 in *La Table Ronde.* Flaubert's protagonist, a former painter, has renounced the use of hashish, and it has become enough for him to sniff the container's odor to have hallucinations. Further, he has noticed that good deeds bring him peace—a sweet, heavenly feeling. "Ainsi le rêve a une influence active, moralisante, sur sa vie—et la vie une influence imaginative sur le rêve" 'Thus, dreaming has an active, moralizing influence on his life—and life an imaginative influence on dreaming.' Finally, Flaubert adds, "la morale est que le bonheur est dans l'*imagination*" 'the moral is that happiness is in the *imagination*.'

Illusion, or perhaps more properly, the belief in an ideal, is, moreover, always associated in Flaubert with decay and corruption. The relationship seems both concomitant and necessary. Thus Emma: "D'où venait donc cette insuffisance de la vie, cette pourriture instantanée des choses où elle s'appuyait?" 'Where did the shortcomings of life come from, that instantaneous decay of everything she leaned on?' Thus Frédéric Moreau, harking back to his youthful visit to the brothel: "C'est là ce que nous avons eu de meilleur!" 'That was the best thing in our lives!' And thus "decadence" in *Salammbô.*

One of the fundamental rules of Flaubert's universe is formulated by the godlike authorial voice that is infrequently but unforgettably heard in *Madame Bovary:* "Il ne faut pas toucher aux idoles: la dorure en reste aux mains" 'One must not handle idols; the gilt rubs off on one's hands.' Failure to heed this injunction leads inevitably to something profounder than disappointment; it leads to disbelief, that is to say, to disillusion. So Emma "retrouvait dans l'adultère toutes les platitudes du mariage" 'in adultery rediscovered all the platitudes of marriage.' Of the Mme Renaud of the 1845 *Education,* the narrator states, "Puis, bien vite elle en [de l'amour] avait eu assez, et le regrettait maintenant" 'Then she quickly had had enough [of love], and regretted it now'; and of Frédéric in the definitive version: "Alors, Frédéric se rappela les jours déjà loin où il enviait l'inexprimable bonheur de se trouver dans une de ces voitures, à côté d'une de ces femmes. Il le possédait, ce bonheur-là, et n'en était pas plus joyeux" 'Then Frédéric remembered the already far-off days when he envied the inexpressible good fortune of riding in one of these carriages, beside one of these women. Now he possessed that good fortune, and was none the happier for it.' And thus *Salammbô*: "Alors elle examina le zaïmph; et quand elle l'eut bien contemplé, elle fut surprise de ne pas avoir ce bonheur qu'elle s'imaginait autrefois. Elle restait mélancolique devant son rêve accompli" 'Then she examined the zaïmph; and when she had looked at it carefully, she was surprised not to feel the happiness that she used to imagine. The realization of her dream left her melancholy.'[22] Thus, possession, incarnation, the actualization of the ideal are deeply balking experiences, and Félicité herself does not escape this paradigm of dashed expectation. When she is permitted to take communion, we read, "Elle la reçut dévotement, mais n'y goûta pas les mêmes délices" (28) 'She received it devoutly, but did not feel the same rapture.' One cannot fail to compare this sense of having been cheated with Félicité's earlier imaginative, nearly fictional identification with Virginie's first communion.

Quand ce fut le tour de Virginie, Félicité se pencha pour la voir; et, avec l'imagination que donnent les vraies tendresses, il lui sembla qu'elle était elle-même cette enfant; sa figure devenait la sienne, sa robe l'habillait, son cœur lui battait dans la poitrine; au moment d'ouvrir la bouche, en fermant les paupières, elle manqua s'évanouir. (28)

When Virginie's turn came, Félicité leaned forward to see her; and, with the imagination that true affection gives, it seemed to her that she herself was that child; her face became hers, she was in her dress, her heart was beating in her breast; and when she opened her mouth and closed her eyelids, she nearly fainted away.

Yet, Félicité does escape to the extent that she does not examine belief, even so superficially as, say, Emma, or scrutinize an

22. Gustave Flaubert, *Madame Bovary*, ed. Claudine Gothot-Mersch (Paris, 1971), 288; Flaubert, *L'Education sentimentale*, in *Œuvres Complètes*, I, 282; Flaubert, *L'Education sentimentale*, ed. Edouard Maynial (Paris, 1964), 209; Flaubert, *Salammbô*, in *Œuvres Complètes*, I, 760.

ideal, like Salammbô, and what really sets her apart is her acceptance of decay—memory under another name. Thus, Loulou may perish (Félicité finds him dead in his cage, like one of the priest's "overthrown idols," "head down"), but his subsequent decay holds nothing disillusioning for Félicité, who makes a cult of decaying relics.

Her room, with the passing of time, comes to resemble a sanctuary. Its prize relics are the shell box (Victor's gift), the illustrated geography book, and Virginie's vermin-eaten "little plush hat!" which finishes the list with an exclamation point. Earlier, when Mme Aubain and Félicité had first ventured to re-enter the dead daughter's room, "des papillons s'envolèrent de l'armoire" (48) 'butterflies flew out of the wardrobe.' There is some mystical significance that attaches to Flaubert's interest in "papillons."[23] In the nightmarish hunt of "Saint Julien," Julien's arrows light harmlessly like white butterflies. Butterflies accompany decisive moments in Emma's sentimental progress in *Madame Bovary*. At the end of Part I, the paper petals from her burning wedding bouquet fly up the chimney like black butterflies. Similarly, another of Emma's most memorable gestures is the view of her synecdochal "nude hand" emerging from the carriage window to scatter the torn pieces of her useless farewell letter to Léon: the pieces settle, like white butterflies, on a field of red clover. And just as Emma cries out, "'Pourquoi, mon Dieu, me suis-je mariée?'" 'Why, my God, did I ever marry?' her thoughts range haphazardly in circles as her dog Djali chases after yellow butterflies. If Victor Hugo is present in the dog's name, which recalls that of Esmeralda's goat, he is also present in the beginning of this scene from "Un Coeur simple" associated with change and decay. It begins, "Elle commençait par regarder tout alentour, pour voir si rien n'avait changé depuis la dernière fois qu'elle était venue" 'She began by looking all around her, to see if anything had changed since the last time she came.' This is an ironic nod to some of Hugo's

---

23. See note 17 above. In the Penguin paperback English edition Robert Baldick translates *papillons* as "moths." Gustave Flaubert, *Three Tales*, trans. Robert Baldick (Harmondsworth, England, 1961), 42.

verses in "Tristesse d'Olympio": "Que peu de temps suffit pour changer toutes choses! . . . Nature au front serein, comme vous oubliez!" 'How little time suffices to change everything! . . . Serene-faced nature, how quickly you forget!'

The fullness of Félicité's room is emphasized by the scene's opening line: "A large wardrobe made the door hard to open." Aside from the Baudelairean note struck by this passage, there is strong internal contrast, for the fullness—some would say the plenitude—of Félicité's room stands in opposition to the emptiness of the house Madame leaves behind. The furniture is gone, the pictures have left unfaded spots on the walls, no trace of Virginie remains. But Félicité's room is Loulou and illumination: "Quelquefois, le soleil entrant par la lucarne frappait son oeil de verre, et en faisait jaillir un grand rayon lumineux qui la mettait en extase" 'Sometimes the sun entering the little window would strike his glass eye, and cause it to emit a great luminous ray that sent her into ecstasy.'

To the enrichment of Félicité's spiritual life (her deafness and declining eyesight are indices of her absorption into inner existence and her slow but steady passage from the human to the otherworldly) corresponds the decay of Félicité's physical surroundings and her detachment from earthly concerns. Her eyes grow weak, the blinds remain closed, the years pass. Fearful of eviction, she asks for no repairs, and the roof leaks onto her bolster. "After Easter she began spitting blood." "Substance," then, shifts from the external to the internal, and from presence to memory and illusion.[24] Loulou becomes the illusory incarnation of the Holy Ghost for Félicité, who contracts the habit of praying to the decaying parrot—and the narrative voice is careful to underscore the coincidence of decay and illusion: "Bien qu'il ne fût pas un cadavre, les vers le dévoraient; une de ses ailes était cassée, l'étoupe lui sortait du ventre. Mais, aveugle à présent,

---

24. Per Nykrog, in "Les *Trois Contes* dans l'évolution de la structure thématique chez Flaubert," *Romantisme*, VI (1973), 55–66, has spoken of this "decline of contact with the exterior counterbalanced by the development of interior life" (62) and related it to the thematics of Flaubert in general.

elle le baisa au front, et le gardait contre sa joue. La Simonne le reprit, pour le mettre sur le reposoir" (69) 'Although he was not a corpse, the worms were eating him up; one of his wings was broken, and the stuffing was coming out of his stomach. But now that she was blind, she kissed him on the forehead and pressed him to her cheek. La Simonne took him away to put him on the altar of repose.'

The world of things decays and rots away, but the realm of illusion subsists. The cascading flowers of the *reposoir* enchase Loulou, and the animal and vegetable are metamorphosed into a Parnassian, mineralized tableau, a reliquary of eternal durability: "Un sucrier en vermeil avait une couronne de voilettes, des pendeloques en pierres d'Alençon brillaient sur de la mousse, deux écrans chinois montraient leurs paysages" 'A silver-gilt sugar bowl was wreathed in violets, some pendants of Alençon stones gleamed on a bed of moss, two Chinese screens displayed their landscapes.' Here the colors previously associated with the parrot—green, pink, blue, and gold (52)—having previously undergone a royal heightening and hardening—from purple to emerald (62–63), for instance, now undergo a final reductive crystallization. Loulou's blue poll is the only part of him that can be spied in the reliquary, and like a precious stone, it is compared to a "plaque de lapis." *Lapis lazuli* was thought to have come to Europe from overseas—"outremer"; thus, *ultra marine* constitutes another link with Loulou's exotic, "blue" origin. Grace descends from the azure mists, the blue country of illusion and poetry.[25] Nowhere in his work has Flaubert so forthrightly emphasized the holy nature of illusion, its *vis conservatrix*, its simultaneous powers of preservation and deliverance.

Yet, any "redemptive" reading of "Un Coeur simple" cannot fail to take into account the paradoxical nature of illusion. If illusion is transfigured into hard, jewel-like imagery in the end, we can never neglect its embodiment in material decay: Loulou's moldering corpse and Virginie's moth-eaten "little plush

25. See Chapter VI.

hat!"²⁶ So we must state, too, that "Un Coeur simple" is an immanent text, seeking its only transcendence (its justification, even its Derridean "presence") in its own intransitive play of signifiers. Flaubert's reversible series, or grand analogies, operate in the mode of tessellations of concordant signifiers. Raymonde Debray-Genette rightly observes that his figures figure only themselves, that they are autoreferential. They generate meanings without arrest or limitation.²⁷ She cites "displacement," that is, a tissue of metonymic relationships, as the basis of construction of the *récit*. But surprisingly, she asserts that the arrival of Loulou is asyndetic, though it obviously forms part of the metonymic "slippage" that she analyzes. The syntagmatic progression, paralleling the psychological transfers of Félicité's loves, would be roughly this: God (<Théodore) > Virginie > Victor > Père Colmiche (himself a synecdoche for other, unspecified loves) > Loulou > the Holy Ghost (=God). That such was Flaubert's method can be confirmed by an early version of the text. This fragment describes Félicité at catechism and introduces the link between the empyrean, the sacred, and the azure: "Ce qui la frappait le plus, c'est l'élément aérien,—le dieu muet, flottant dans l'air, se perdant dans le ciel, dans l'azur—l'oiseau" 'What would strike her the most is the aerial element—the unspeaking god, floating in the air, disappearing into the sky, into the azure—the bird.'²⁸

It would be tempting to claim that the final scene of "Un Coeur simple" lies somewhere between the signifier and the sacred, that it establishes a linguistic state of grace.²⁹ By forcing the text a bit, it would be possible to assert that Félicité experi-

---

26. Compare the "decadent" world of Salammbô's jewelry. Flaubert, *Salammbô*, in *Œuvres Complètes*, I, 758. In a slightly less erotically charged scene, Charles had contemplated Emma sewing: on her shoulders little beads of perspiration form. Flaubert, *Madame Bovary*, 23.

27. Raymonde Debray-Genette, "Les Figures du récit dans "Un Coeur simple,'" *Poétique*, I (1970), 364.

28. Willenbrink, *The Dossier of Flaubert's "Un Coeur simple,"* 203.

29. Karl Uitti has said: "In Flaubert's work a kind of theory of language is poeticized: the principles of linguistic mediation are themselves celebrated in this complex cluster of related signs." Uitti, "Figures and Fiction: Linguistic Deformation in the Novel," *Kentucky Romance Quarterly*, XVII (1970), 167. In a seriocomic vein, the narrator

ences the apotheosis of Loulou through Mère Simonne's nar-
rative-descriptive act. Indeed, to relieve Félicité's concern for
the parrot ("Est-il bien?" 'Is he all right?' she asks), la Simonne
mounts a chair to observe and relay an account of the procession
through the focusing agent of the *oeil-de-boeuf*. It could then be
claimed that the end of the tale is an implied mediated description of the Corpus Christi feast, a micromodule of the narrative
act, an embedded tale gesturing towards literarity. (And earlier
we saw that Félicité derives more satisfaction from mediation
than participation.)

The text does not justify such a reading. As has often been re-
marked, the chief Flaubertian stylistic agent of reader-character
identification, free indirect discourse—what should be called
stylistic syllepsis—is relatively absent from "Un Coeur simple."
Surely this absence is revealing. Félicité is for observation, not
for absorption. Her world is sympathetic yet remote, disjointed
yet harmonious, and thoroughly ambiguous in its final exaltation. Flaubert took time off from *Bouvard et Pécuchet* to compose
his *Trois Contes*. Returning to his pair of idiots, he perhaps gave
them the definitive statement on belief; when Bouvard scoffs at
the sight of their servant Marcel kneeling in prayer, Pécuchet's
rejoinder is this: "Qu'importe la croyance! Le principal est de
croire" 'What does the belief matter! The important thing is to
believe.'[30]

---

of Julian Barnes's novel, *Flaubert's Parrot* (London, 1984), pursues this linguistic connection: "You could say that the parrot, representing clever vocalisation without much
brain power, was Pure Word. If you were a French academic, you might say that he was
un symbole de Logos" (p. 18).

30. Flaubert, *Bouvard et Pécuchet*, in *Œuvres Complètes*, II, 289.

IX ~ The Blue Illusion of Alphonse Daudet's

Fromont jeune et Risler aîné

In 1872, only two years before the publication of *Fromont jeune et Risler aîné,* the novel that has been said to mark Alphonse Daudet's evolution from ironist to realist, the author of *Lettres de mon moulin* and *Tartarin* began to meet regularly for literary discussions with Flaubert, Turgenev, Edmond de Goncourt, and Zola.[1] These meetings were to be decisive for Daudet's practice of realism in the novel, despite Daudet's somewhat humorous picture of his friends ("Nous ne nous vendrons jamais, nous autres!" 'We will never sell!'). It is under the lingering Realist influence that Daudet was to claim in *Histoire de mes livres* that all his characters and settings were always drawn from life: he said they were "strictly true settings and types, copied straight from nature. From nature! That's been my sole method of working."[2]

Daudet goes on to assert that all the characters of *Fromont jeune* were based on life models, citing specifically Old Gardinois, Planus, Sidonie, Risler, and Delobelle. Documentation came in a variety of forms: close observation of the Marais quar-

1. Murray Sachs, *The Career of Alphonse Daudet* (Cambridge, Mass., 1965), 82.
2. See introduction to Alphonse Daudet, *Fromont jeune et Risler aîné*, Volume V of Daudet, *Œuvres Complètes illustrées* (20 vols.; Paris, 1929), 2. All page references in the text are to this edition.

ter, where Daudet was living at the time; a dinner at the Palais-Royal with his family, which became the background for the catastrophic outing of Risler and Planus at the end of the novel; a trip to the outskirts of Paris for the Montrouge setting of Planus' house and the panoramic site of Risler's suicide. One should mention also a somewhat neglected aspect of Daudet's realism (perhaps in the category of "choses vues" 'things seen'), namely his portrayal of what he calls in *Sapho* "les vertes stations des bords de la Seine" 'the green stations of the banks of the Seine,' the small towns an easy train ride away from Paris. These are the *banlieue* settings to which numbers of Daudet characters take holiday outings turned out in their Sunday best ("l'endimanchement—cette fête du pauvre" 'Sunday best—the poor man's celebration').[3] The small, detached houses and garden plots and the dust convey perfectly the aspirations and disappointments of the petits bourgeois and point to their acquisitiveness, to the seemingly permanent French passion for freeholdry, reflected yet today in the quest for the *résidence secondaire*.

The reader feels, though, that the authenticity of milieu and of the characters' sources is not replicated at the narrational level (in either plot or style) and that such "realism" scarcely prevents the characters from foundering on the rocks of their illusions. To take only the question of money—usually a revealing matter in a Realistic novel, as seen in its devastating role in any tale of debt, speculation, or usury by Balzac or Zola—one can hardly say that it poses any difficulty at all in *Fromont jeune et Risler aîné*. For there is income aplenty; its squandering rather than its scarcity is the real problem. When the firm's debts of a hundred thousand francs fall due, they are met on exceedingly short notice—overnight—through the realization of the characters' assets—Sidonie's diamond necklace and the house in Asnières. There is simply none of the grim financial despair that Balzac had accustomed readers to. Indeed, the whole notion of *échéances*—the payment date—comes to fruition in the most overtly "fantastic" episode of the novel, the "Légende fantas-

3. Alphonse Daudet, *Sapho*, Volume X of Daudet, *Œuvres Complètes illustrées*, 22, 188–89.

tique du petit homme bleu" 'Fantastic Legend of the Little Blue Man,' which opens the fourth and final division of *Fromont jeune et Risler aîné*. The concept of having to "pay" or "own up" in both financial and moral senses coalesces in the elfin personality of this shrill-voiced imp, who scuttles by night from rooftop to chimney pot crying "L'échéance!" to the restless debtors of Paris. Thus, the various *échéances*, which have been building throughout the novel, are gathered in a skein of fantasy or folklore rather than in the tenebrous realistic mode that one might have expected. Although Sidonie is certainly exposed and humiliated in the course of this chapter, one can hardly assert that she gets her comeuppance here, any more than she did earlier when Frantz returns to Paris in a chapter ironically entitled "Le justicier" 'The Justicer.' Sidonie simply finds another stage and moves on to a more visible and literal plane of deception with her new career as a cabaret artiste.

Structurally, one can also discern a pseudo-Realistic linearity. The opening scene is a dramatic presentation of all the principals at the wedding reception of Risler and Sidonie. The arrangement seems to be typically Balzacian. The drama behind the first scene is hinted at, but its latent significance is developed only subsequently, through a series of flashbacks that eventually rejoin the "present" time of the work and then continue through to its denouement. But the development of events in Daudet's novel in no way resembles a relentless Balzacian sequence. The flashbacks constitute more of a series of tableau-like entries and exits which tend to interrupt the flow of the action. In consequence, there is little of the inexorable and the implacable, the unstemmable tide of events leading to a crisis. But the *petit homme bleu* episode is there to prove that such was Daudet's purpose, and it shows that the gates to *Fromont jeune et Risler aîné* are made of ivory and not of horn. Illusion, paradoxically, is the very substance of this novel.

Illusions: the lifelike poses of the "oiseaux et mouches pour modes" 'fashion birds and flies' so lovingly crafted by the pathetic, lame Désirée; the amorous idyll of Claire Fromont, plunged into a dream of maternity while she is cruelly deceived by her husband; Chèbe's empty store, with its nonexistent Commission-Exportation; Risler's dream of being an inventor (again, Risler's "dodecagon rotary press" lacks the intensity of the Balzacian *recherche de l'absolu*);[4] but most of all "l'Illustre Delobelle" the ham actor, a character of such compelling interest that he threatens to usurp the leading role of the novel.[5] Henry James and Zola both recognized Delobelle as the most successful character in the book. Delobelle merits careful attention.

Although Delobelle is sincerely grieved by the impending death of his daughter, Désirée, he does not give up his daily *flâneries* (strolls), which have become an integral part of that marvelous theatrical mission that, by common family acclaim, "he does not have the right to renounce." So long has this *cabotin* played at being what he is not (and one of his favorite roles is that of *Ruy Blas*) that he is incapable of seeing himself as he really is—the very embodiment of *bovarysme*. He becomes the Suffering Father with friends who ask after Désirée's health: "Reading his soul, no one could have said where true and feigned grief separated, so intermingled were they" (272). Désirée herself, upon her very deathbed, cannot quite bring herself, even for her mother's sake, to ask her father to give up his illusion of becoming a great actor. (In a sense he has already attained his greatest role.) In a trailing voice, she can do no more than ask him to "give up"; the great man half understands her uncompleted last request and simultaneously refuses to comprehend. All of Delobelle's actor friends (here the French *comédien* is much more expressive than the English *actor*) attend Désirée's funeral. They attend out of friendship for Delobelle, but also in the equally fervent hope of seeing their names quoted in newspaper accounts of the ceremony. Madame Delobelle herself will not attend the burial service (no doubt she must continue to slave away in order to support the great man's illusory career), but

---

4. In Daudet's notes, Risler is intent on inventing colors, "un certain *bleu cobalt* qui le poursuit" (italics added) 'a certain *cobalt blue* that obsesses him.' Compare Désirée's "pays bleu" of Flaubertian origin, and see Chapter VI.

5. Delobelle was inspired, perhaps, by Flaubert's *cabotin*, Delmare. Certainly the scene of the café chantant, discussed below, is reminiscent, in its phony Moorish decor, of the Alhambra dancehall in *L'Education sentimentale*.

Delobelle will lead off the procession: "En tête marchait De-lobelle, secoué par les sanglots, s'attendrissant presque autant sur lui-même, pauvre père enterrant son enfant, que sur sa fille morte" (273) 'At the head marched Delobelle, racked with sobs, pitying himself—a poor father burying his child—almost as much as his dead daughter.'

Into this character—compelling despite his murderous ego-tism—is decanted a deep part of the complex and double per-sonality of Alphonse Daudet himself.

> *Homo duplex, Homo duplex!* la première fois que je me suis aperçu que j'étais deux, à la mort de mon frère Henri, quand papa criait si dra-matiquement: "il est mort! il est mort!" mon premier MOI pleurait, et le second pensait: "Quel cri juste! Que ce serait beau au théâtre!" J'avais quatorze ans.[6]

> *Homo duplex, Homo duplex!* the first time I realized that I was really two persons was when my brother Henri died; Father was crying so dramati-cally: "He's dead! he's dead!" My first self was weeping, and the second was thinking: "How right that sounds! How beautiful it would be in the theater!" I was fourteen.

Alongside the double man, Daudet has also set the double woman, or rather the woman who has split into two characters. In effect, in the working notes for *Fromont jeune*, we find that Sidonie was first called Désirée. (The present Désirée did not yet exist.) She was also called Amélie Lefèvre, and when the name Sidonie was decided upon, the name Amélie was shifted for a time to the character now known as Claire.[7] Thus, we could actually speak of a *mulier triplex*, which would perhaps explain why *Fromont jeune et Risler aîné* lacks the polar, Balzacian opposition between the Madame de Mortsaufs and the Lady Dudleys, the Paulines ("l'être incré, tout esprit, tout amour" 'the uncreated being, all spirit, all love') and the Foedoras (ego-tistical incarnations of society).[8] It also explains why the dream-er's role (before the great café chantant scene) seems not to fit a

---

6. Alphonse Daudet, *Notes sur la vie*, Volume I of Daudet, *Œuvres Complètes illustrées*, 16, quoted in Sachs, *The Career of Alphonse Daudet*, 15.

7. Chèbe was called M. Rameau; and before finally becoming Risler, the title char-acter was originally Chardon, the name of Balzac's exemplar of illusion.

8. Daudet's Claire-Sidonie opposition, of course, is that of "real and fake pearls."

character so base and scheming as Sidonie: the dreamer's portion has been largely shared out to Désirée. The shift explains why early passages such as this one do not seem to be followed up: "Sidonie fell asleep . . . and began a beautiful dream that was to last for her whole youth and cost her many tears." And finally, another link between these characters is Désirée's sobriquet—"Zizi"—which returns hauntingly in Sidonie's exotic creole song of lost love.

> Pauv' pitit mam'zelle Zizi
> C'est l'amou, l'amou qui tourne
> La tête à li
>
> Poor little mam'zelle Zizi;
> Love, love is turning
> Her head

We must now turn to Sidonie's form of illusion. Early on, Sidonie is associated with the illusory and the synthetic; two early chapters devoted to the "Histoire de la petite Chèbe" 'The Little Chèbe Girl's Story' are subtitled "Les perles fausses" 'The Fake Pearls' and "Les vers luisants" 'The Glowworms.' She is apprenticed to a certain Mlle Le Mire (*mirer* means "to look at" in slang) in an atelier of costume jewelry where "on ne travaillait que dans le faux, le clinquant, et c'est bien là que la petite Chèbe devait faire l'apprentissage de sa vie" (41) 'they only fabricated fakes and tinsel, and it was there indeed that the little Chèbe girl was to learn about life.'[9] Sidonie's world of artifice is resumed in the very world that she grows up in, that of the ubiquitous "article de Paris" 'Paris souvenir' of Marais fabrication. Sidonie is destined to become a petit bourgeois version— and a particularly vicious one—of the *femme sans coeur*. When, exposed by Risler, she leaves their apartment, her presence lingers on in the shelf of tacky figurines and bibelots that remains behind: "The shelf was like Sidonie's soul."

In the end, there are two forms of illusion in *Fromont jeune et Risler aîné*. There is the noble form—the "pays bleu" 'blue land'

9. Irresistibly, one is drawn to compare this sweatshop with the one later portrayed in *L'Assommoir*, where the adolescent Nana finishes off a not so different kind of apprenticeship.

of Désirée, which is also Claire's and the two Rislers'—and the vulgar, nomadic, or Bohemian (Daudet's term) form, the chosen land of Sidonie, of "l'Illustre Delobelle," and perhaps most of all of a thoroughly suspect and important, though minor, character, "a certain Cazabon, called Cazaboni, an Italian tenor from Toulouse."

The reader has his best glimpse of this Cazaboni in the scruffy setting of the café chantant, whose decor is the perfect expression of shop-soiled Romanticism: "des colonnes dorées, une décoration mauresque, rouge vif, bleu tendre, avec de petits croissants et des turbans roulés en ornement" 'gilt columns, a Moorish decor in bright red and baby blue, with little crescents and wound turbans.' In this stifling room where the neighborhood shopkeepers "avec leurs dames et leurs demoiselles" 'with their wives and daughters' are crowded together, Cazaboni, Sidonie's new lover, makes his splendid appearance. The spectators' "imaginations de boutique" 'shopkeepers' imaginations' quiver to his song, which this pomaded Tartarin delivers in full evening dress.

> Mes beaux lions aux crins dorés
> Du sang des troupeaux altérés,
> Halte-là! . . . Je fais *sentinellô!*
>
> My fine lions with your golden manes,
> Sated on the blood of the flocks,
> Stop right there! . . . I stand *sentinellô!*

And Cazabon *dit Cazaboni* seems to dart a scornful glance at his public of tranquil *épiciers* and to issue a challenge to each male in the room: "Ce n'est pas toi qui serais capable de faire *sentinellô* à la barbe des lions et en habit noir encore, et avec des gants jaunes" '*You* wouldn't be up to standing *sentinellô* right in the lion's beard and, what's more, in formal dress, with yellow gloves.'

Risler aîné dies from the discovery of Frantz's betrayal, but he dies just as much from the clash between the two worlds that we have examined: on one hand, that of the "lion tamers" and the "pauv' pitit mam'zelle Zizi" and, on the other, a world less false but more pedestrian, more "realistic"—that of the dodecagon rotary presses, which win prizes at the Manchester industrial fair. Daudet writes that Sidonie is "not one of those sentimental women à la Bovary," and indeed from *Madame Bovary* to *Fromont jeune et Risler aîné* the meanings of illusion and of its sequel have evolved into a new phase. Emma's ideal will succumb under the weight of Homaisian platitudes, which have the last word. Sidonie, flanked by Cazaboni, Madame Dobson, and the "blooming and sonorous Delobelle,"[10] will leave this stage for another one, for a repeat performance. She will have gained a victory, though facile, over a petit bourgeois world whose only crime is to be inadequate, to dream a dream too modest (the efficient manufacturing of cheap wallpaper) to measure itself even with the degraded dream of Sidonie.

Alphonse Daudet himself, in his autobiographical *Trente Ans de Paris*, was highly conscious of the "singular" mixture of realism and fantasy that pervades his works. Writing of himself in the third person ("D..."), he put it this way: "Quand il fait un livre d'observation, une étude de moeurs bourgeoises, il s'y trouve toujours un côté fantastique, poétique" 'When he composes a book of observation, a study of bourgeois manners, it always contains a fantastical and poetic element.'

10. The phrase is Henry James's, from his "Alphonse Daudet," in *Partial Portraits* (London, 1888), 224. James's appreciation of Daudet's gift for caricatural observation has its negative counterpart in Croce's later accusation that Daudet's characters are "static; they do not change in the novel, which serves only to exhibit and portray them in so many particular scenes; they are almost caricatures or mock characters." Benedetto Croce, "Zola e Daudet," *La Critica*, XIX (1921), 200.

X   The Mirror of Artifice: Maupassant's

Bel-Ami

For many readers *Bel-Ami* is essentially a novel to be read through a series of Balzacian (and Stendhalian) intertexts, an approach seemingly authorized by Maupassant himself: "J'ai voulu raconter la vie d'un aventurier pareil à tous ceux que nous côtoyons chaque jour. . . . Voulant analyser une crapule, je l'ai développée dans un milieu digne d'elle" 'I wished to recount the life of an adventurer like those we rub elbows with every day. . . . Seeking to analyze a scoundrel, I developed him in a milieu worthy of him.'[1] That milieu is the corrupt world of journalism, where reporting the news is incidental to financial manipulations, for in a punning phrase, one of the collaborators of *La Vie Française* states that the paper's purpose is to "[naviguer] sur les fonds de l'Etat et sur les bas-fonds de la politique" '[sail] on the funds / depths of the State and the lower depths / funds of politics.' The reader of nineteenth-century fiction will think of the journalists in *Illusions perdues* and *La Peau de chagrin*, with the difference that the actresses, the Euphrasies and Coralies of Balzac have been replaced by professional prostitutes and prostituted *femmes du monde*.

1. Guy de Maupassant, "Aux critiques de *Bel-Ami:* Une Réponse," *Gil Blas*, July 7, 1885, cited in André Vial, *Guy de Maupassant et l'art du roman* (Paris, 1954).

As for the rise of the adventurer, Georges Duroy neatly passes for a Third Republic Rastignac whose exploits allow one to establish this thumbnail morphology of the *arriviste* tale: a penniless young provincial arrives in Paris where a series of benefactors (adjuvants) initiates him into the life of the capital. He receives disabused, if not cynical, advice from an older and wiser mentor figure. The women he meets are somehow associated with the opera or the music hall. He decides to exploit his success with women to rise in the world, in the course of which he has dealings with a shady banker, is involved in a challenge and a duel, and marries the daughter of his former mistress. He becomes a *député et ministre*. It goes without saying that he ends up immensely rich and respected.

If Maupassant is constructing a variation on this theme, then perhaps the interest of the novel lies in the particular coding process—or recoding process—that has been adapted or updated for the reader of half a century after *Le Père Goriot*. The interest of Balzac's novel lies in a suspense of sorts, the deferred knowledge of whether Eugène will or will not "kill the mandarin," or perhaps in learning when he will traverse his "Parisian Rubicon." And if corruption of innocence is the essential semic kernel of this type of novel, then prostitution is its apt but rather obvious figuration in *Bel-Ami*. Yet, prostitution is not a point or stage to which Georges Duroy ultimately sinks; it is rather his point of departure, for he is introduced as a typed character: "Grand, bien fait, blond . . . il ressemblait au mauvais sujet des romans populaires" 'Tall, handsome, blond . . . he resembled the ne'er-do-well of popular novels.'[2] His milieu is that of Parisian low life, figured physically in the following passage, which gives us what we might call the atmospherics of the novel.

C'était une de ces soirées d'été où l'air manque dans Paris. La ville, chaude comme une étuve, paraissait suer dans la nuit étouffante. Les égouts soufflaient par leurs bouches de granit leurs haleines empestées, et

2. Guy de Maupassant, *Bel-Ami* (Paris, 1968), 8. All page references in the text are to this edition.

les cuisines souterraines jetaient à la rue, par leurs fenêtres basses, les miasmes inflâmes des eaux de vaisselle et des vieilles sauces. (8)

It was an airless summer evening in Paris. The city, hot as a steam-room, seemed to sweat in the stifling night. The sewers exhaled their stinking breath through their granite mouths, and underground kitchens pumped foul odors of dishwater and rancid sauces through their low windows.[3]

This is Duroy's chosen milieu, "les milieux où grouillent les filles publiques" 'the places where prostitutes swarm,' and indeed Chapter 1 ends with his being taken home by a prostitute—at a discount price.

Prostitution—aside from being, of course, a social, economic, and political phenomenon of the age—is a simulacrum of love. It points to an appearance without substance, to a crude desire disguising an inauthenticity or hollowness at the core of a certain type of human relationship. It is thus an appropriate signifier for a code of artificial gestures pointing not to a something—for example, to the essence of the character of Georges Duroy—but to an ontological lack, to an image of nothingness.

This, it seems to me, is the code that Maupassant has chosen to figure his narration. And though prostitution appears to lie at the (hollow) thematic core of the book—and there is admittedly a recognition scene of sorts in which Duroy is presented as the kindred soul of a famous *courtisane* ("il y avait quelque chose de commun entre eux . . . ils étaient de même race, de même âme" [169] 'they had something in common . . . they were of the same race and soul')—the evocations of prostitution are but one actualization of a matrix concept that commands event and image in *Bel-Ami*. This concept might be called artifice, illusion, or vacancy.

I propose now to pinpoint a number of these foci of facticity. The most patent one has already been mentioned: the news-

---

3. The "sauce" (which disguises an essential rancidity) returns when Madeleine Forestier prepares Duroy's first newspaper article ("Souvenirs d'un chasseur d'Afrique" 'Memories of an African Hunter': "Oui, je vous arrangerai la chose. Je ferai la sauce, mais il me faut le plat" (50) 'Yes, I'll fix it up for you. I'll do the sauce, but you'll have to furnish the dish.'

paper so obviously and ominously named *La Vie Française*. In this world of imaginary interviews conducted by a certain "Saint-Potin" 'Holy Gossip,' the most prestigious beat is perhaps that of the *échotier* (brief news items), and the sign of professional expertise lies in the mastery of a banal spindle-and-ball game called *le bilboquet* (something akin to the yo-yo or the hula hoop of later years). Skill in *bilboquet* confers a "sort of superiority in the newspaper offices" (150). The use of the *bilboquet* was apparently widespread enough for poet and humorist Charles Cros, with his usual tongue-in-cheek mordancy, to have devoted one of his monologues to it. It is dedicated to Coquelin Cadet, a champion performer of such texts, and in it the utter absurdity of the talent of the *bilboquétiste* is also assimilated to nullity. The narrator tells of encountering a crowd of Parisians surrounding a young herbalist, a virtuoso of the *bilboquet*. He makes twenty, thirty successful passes, catching the ball on the spindle, then the spindle on the ball. In mock exasperation the narrator steps forward from the crowd to stop the display. He admonishes the young man for using inferior equipment; he should use only the best English, German, Italian, Belgian, Dutch, and Portuguese balls, cords, and spindles. He must dedicate himself, like the narrator, to a strict training regimen; he must give up his trade in medicinal herbs and practice for ten or twenty years: "Vous ne saurez rien. Ne perdez pas courage, continuez, et vous ne saurez rien! rien! rien!" 'You'll know nothing. Don't give up, keep going, and you'll know nothing! nothing! nothing!' And when the astonished young *herboriste* makes to hand over his *bilboquet* so that this maestro might demonstrate, the latter reacts with fury.

"Ah! je lui ai répondu: Croyez-vous que je me sers d'un pareil bâton de chaise? et dans la rue encore. . . . Se montrer comme un chanteur des cours? Ce serait perdre toute dignité artistique. (*Au public.*) Je ne voudrais même pas jouer ici, parce que j'aurais honte de plaire, vu mon absolue nullité! car je suis nul! je ne sais rien! je suis nul! nul! nul! . . . je ne sais rien, rien, rien!!! (*Il sort les bras levés, exaspéré.*)"[4]

4. Jacques Brenner, *Charles Cros*, Collection Poètes d'aujourd hui (Paris, 1963), 145–46.

"Ah!" I replied to him. "Do you think I use an old stick of chair wood like that? Right out on a public street. . . . Show myself like a street singer? I'd lose all my artistic dignity. (*To the public.*) I wouldn't even want to play here, because I'd be ashamed of pleasing, given my absolute nullity! For I'm nothing! I'm a zero! a zero! a zero!!! (*He leaves with arms raised in exasperation.*)"

Charles Cros's intent, like Maupassant's, is to expose to contempt and mockery an essentially empty talent, and both do so by putting a trivial, absurd activity at the very center of stupid admiration, in one case that of the circle of street gawkers and in the other that of the newsroom. A nothing—or a nullity—is enough to seduce the crowd.

Appropriately enough for a novel foregrounding and valorizing pure appearance, mirrors play an important role in the stages of Duroy's successful rise. On the evening of the very first dinner party he attends at the Forestiers, a series of mirrors greets him at every landing of his climb to the third-floor apartment. On the first floor Duroy recoils, startled by the image of a gentleman in evening dress: "Puis il demeurait stupéfait: c'était lui-même, reflété par une haute glace en pied" (28) 'Then he stood still in astonishment: it was himself reflected in a full-length mirror.' Thus, he is delighted to allay his worries by discovering that he looks altogether chic in his rented costume. He takes a moment to rehearse his appearance.

Alors il s'étudia comme font les acteurs pour apprendre leurs rôles. Il se sourit, se tendit la main, fit des gestes, exprima des sentiments: l'étonnement, le plaisir, l'approbation; et il chercha les degrés du sourire et les intentions de l'oeil pour se montrer galant auprès des dames, leur faire comprendre qu'on les admire et qu'on les désire. (28)

Then he studied himself the way actors do to learn their roles. He smiled to himself, held out his hand, made gestures and expressed surprise, pleasure, and approval; and he sought various types of smiles and eye expressions to be gallant to the ladies, to make them understand that they are admired and desired.

The Stendhalian intertext resonates here as we think of Julien observing the young Bishop of Agde practicing his motions of benediction before *his* full-length mirror—significantly termed a *psyché*. Maupassant has trebled the mirror imagery: Duroy sees his reflection again in another mirror on the second floor: "Et une confiance immodérée en lui-même emplit son âme. Certes, il réussirait avec cette figure-là et son désir d'arriver" (29) 'And an immoderate self-confidence filled his soul. Of course he would succeed with that air and his ambition.' He bounds with joy to the third-floor mirror, twists his moustache, smooths his hair, and, just before ringing the apartment bell, pronounces these words: "Voilà une excellente invention" (29) 'What an excellent invention.' Thus, the mirrors of this early scene are anticipatory, and Duroy's progressive confidence in his image, in the mask that he projects ("Of course he would succeed with that air") as he climbs the three floors is a proleptic micromodule of his social ascendancy.

A mirror reflects not the object or person itself, but rather an image; it projects a distortion of that object or person. Duroy is thus figured as a mask, as a performance, as an artificial creation: "Voilà une excellente invention." Duroy will be seen to continue to pay homage to his own image in a series of mirrors—and in rare moments of self-doubt he seeks reassurance in his mirror. Mirrors are mentioned in at least ten separate scenes in *Bel-Ami*, and one of them confirms his triumph: "Voilà des millionnaires qui passent" 'See the millionaires passing by,' says Duroy as he and Madeleine return home after settling the matter of Vaudrec's legacy. What is remarkable about this particular instance is that the text is at pains to emphasize the ephemerality of the moment. The gas in the stairway has been turned off, and so Duroy pronounces his triumphant phrase while striking a match in front of the first-floor mirror. But the narrator asserts the pair's insubstantiality: "They looked like ghosts, suddenly visible and ready to disappear into the night" (369). The text thus foregrounds the fragility of the entire referential structure upon which it supposedly reposes, since the mirror no longer reflects a set of stable referents. And this gap between signifier and signifieds explains the valorization of appearance. Seeming and being, or the disjunction of the two, lies at the heart of the whole process of nomination in this scene.

All of the female protagonists of *Bel-Ami* may also be assimilated to this code of appearances because of their propensity and preference for the artificial. Clotilde de Marelle, Duroy's steady mistress, of whom he becomes the "kept man," has a pronounced taste for costumes. She likes to disguise herself as a working-class girl or a schoolboy, and to drag Duroy into cheap bars and dance halls—a *guinguette*, a *bastringue*, or a *caboulot:* "Alors commença une série d'excursions dans tous les endroits louches où s'amuse le peuple" (118) 'Then began a series of excursions into all the low-life places where the lower classes entertain themselves.' For she admits to having "des goûts canaille" (117) 'low tastes.' The theatricality of her costumes is also stressed. Dressed like a *soubrette de vaudeville*, she imagines that she is thoroughly disguised, whereas in reality she is hidden "in the manner of ostriches." Her exits on these occasions are theatrical as well: "Elle filait vivement, la tête basse, d'un pas menu, d'un pas d'actrice qui quitte la scène" (119) 'She would leave swiftly with lowered head and tiny steps, the steps of an actress leaving the stage.'

Madeleine Forestier, the talented ghostwriter whom Duroy marries in order to consolidate his position at the newspaper, is another woman whose tastes are for the artificial. When she and Duroy decide to spend their honeymoon in Normandy with his parents, he warns her that they are not make-believe peasants: "You know, they're peasants, country peasants, not comic opera ones" (249). Despite this admonition, Madeleine is ill at ease; she would have liked the parents to be "more like in books, perhaps, nobler, more affectionate and picturesque" (256). In the end the natural world of the countryside only increases her discomfort, and a walk in the forest absolutely terrifies her.

Un frisson singulier lui passa dans l'âme et lui courut sur la peau; une angoisse confuse lui serra le coeur. Pourquoi? Elle ne comprenait pas. Mais il lui semblait qu'elle était perdue, noyée, entourée de périls, abandonnée de tous, seule, seule au monde sous cette voûte vivante qui frémissait là-haut. (259)

A strange shiver passed through her soul and ran over her skin; a confused distress gripped her heart. Why? She didn't understand. But it seemed to her that she was lost, drowned, surrounded by dangers, deserted, alone, alone in the world under that living canopy rustling overhead.

Her mood changes when the newlyweds decide to return early to Paris, where they tenderly embrace during a reassuring carriage ride through the domesticated nature of the Bois de Boulogne. Madeleine proclaims her relief.

Te rappelles-tu la forêt de chez toi, comme c'était sinistre. Il me semblait qu'elle était pleine de bêtes affreuses et qu'elle n'avait pas de bout. Tandis qu'ici, c'est charmant. On sent des caresses dans le vent, et je sais bien que Sèvres est de l'autre côté du Bois. (275)

Do you remember the forest near your home? How sinister it was. To me it seemed endless and full of nasty animals. But this is charming. One can feel a caress in the breeze, and I know that Sèvres is just on the other side of the park.

Nature is the uncontrolled other, the undefinable, whereas the Bois is a euphemized, artificial, limitable analogue of it.

Finally, even the pure, young Suzanne Walter finds pleasure in make-believe, for during her elopement with, or rather sequestering by Duroy, she plays at being a shepherdess. In addition, he passes her off as his sister (an old *vaudeville* situation), and they live chastely in a sort of amorous camaraderie. After the father's legal consent to the marriage is obtained, they must return to Paris: "Déjà," laments the still undeflowered bride-to-be, "ça m'amusait tant d'être votre femme!" (430) 'Already! I was having such fun being your wife!'

Milieus, like characters, are coded to the artificial in *Bel-Ami*. The interiors of both houses where Duroy is received are constantly assimilated to a hothouse, the *serre*, to the point that the atmospheres are virtually interchangeable. First, there is the piano in the Forestier household: on it stand two strange shrubs, one covered with red blossoms, the other with white. They "avaient l'air de *plantes factices*, invraisemblables, trop belles pour être vraies. L'air était frais et pénétré d'un parfum vague, doux, qu'on n'aurait pu définir, dont on ne pouvait dire le nom" (40; italics added) 'looked like *artificial plants*, unreal, too beautiful to be true. The air was cool and suffused with a sweetish, vague aroma that was undefinable and nameless.' Then there is the *serre* in the Walter mansion: It harbors "de grands arbres des pays chauds abritant des massifs de fleurs rares. . . . C'était une étrange sensation douce, malsaine et charmante, de *nature factice*, énervante et molle" (379; italics added) 'tall tropical trees sheltering beds of rare flowers. . . . The sensation was sweetish, unhealthy, and pleasant, of an *artificial nature*, enervating and soft.' The common elements from both interiors—the strange and sweetish odor, the exotic plants, the vaguely unhealthy hothouse atmosphere, are synthesized in the adjective *factice*—in both instances the collateral signifier of inauthenticity.

Insalubrity and artificed nature are conjoined on the occasion of the *assaut*, a fencing demonstration organized for the ostensible benefit of the "orphans of the sixth arrondissement." This social event draws the beau monde but packs them into a particularly unpleasant setting. A fetid atmosphere exudes from an underground *salle d'armes* built for two hundred persons but into which nearly four hundred attempt to force their way. From below, a whiff of warm dampness rises, along with the smell of incense, reminiscent of church services, and women's perfumes: verbena, iris, and violets. The room itself has been disguised as a natural setting: "Toute la cave était illuminée avec des guirlandes de gaz et des lanternes vénitiennes cachées en des feuillages qui voilaient les murs de pierre salpêtrés. On ne voyait rien que des branchages. Le plafond était garni de fougères, le sol couvert de feuilles et de fleurs" (291) 'The whole cellar was lighted with garlands of gas jets and Venetian lanterns hidden in foliage that concealed the whitewashed walls, so that only greenery was visible. The ceiling was draped with ferns, and the floor strewn with leaves and flowers.'

The grand demonstration match of the day opposes two female fencers ("Grrrrande surprise") wearing tights and half skirts. Their performance excites the natural taste of Parisian audiences "pour les gentilesses un peu polissonnes, pour les élégances du genre canaille, pour le faux-joli et le faux-gracieux, les chanteuses de café-concert et les couplets d'opérette" (297) 'for slightly risqué niceties, for low elegance, for the pseudo-smart and the pseudoelegant, for revue chanteuses and musical comedy songs.'

Finally, let us turn to the denouement of *Bel-Ami*, the ceremonial scene that pulls together, to a very broad degree, the network of signifiers that up to now I have variously labeled illusion, disguise, and artifice. This synthesis comes on the wedding day of Duroy—by now le Baron Du Roy de Cantel—and Suzanne Walter. The marriage is celebrated in the church of the Madeleine, and the entire scene is treated under the sign of *spectacle*. It is a veritable pageant of the parvenu. So many uninvited spectators linger for the show that the police are required for crowd control. Early comers seek out the best seats to witness the ceremonies. The marriage actually begins with the traditional *trois coups* (three warning knocks) of a theatrical performance: "Tout à coup le suisse frappa trois fois le pavé du bois de sa hallebarde" (439) 'All at once the beadle struck the stone floor three times with the wooden butt of his halberd.' The bride comes walking down the aisle looking not so much like a real woman as an imitation of one: "a delicious white plaything . . . a miniature bride." The groomsmen march in perfect step, as if they had been choreographed by a ballet master (439). The union is blessed by the "new bishop of Tangiers," an intratextual allusion to the grand financial manipulation that had been organized by Duroy's father-in-law and is the source of Duroy's immense fortune. Organs play, there is a performance by two singers brought specially over from the opera, and the *serre*-like odor, that is, the *benjoin* (incense) burning at the altar envelops the two thousand guest-spectators. The couple emerges onto the parvis of the church, where Duroy's glance is drawn immediately across the Seine—Rastignac-like—to the next theater of his triumphal ascent, the Chambre des Députés. (M. Walter has predicted that he will become "député et ministre" one day.) Finally, the last sentence of the novel returns us to eroticism and to that insistent gauge of Duroy's rise, the mirror, for Duroy ends thinking of the image of "Mme de Marelle rajustant en face de la glace les petits cheveux frisés de ses tempes, toujours défaits au sortir du lit" (445) 'Mme de Marelle in front of the mirror, arranging the little curls around her temples, which were always mussed when she got out of bed.'

Barthes wrote of the *effet de réel* that its purpose was to achieve redundancy, or textual saturation, in such a way as to send this signal to the reader: "I am the real."[5] The effect would be to achieve a verisimilitude of the unmotivated detail. As we have seen, *Bel-Ami* poses a challenge to the concept advanced by Barthes, Philippe Hamon,[6] and others—that the Realist text aims at maximum lisibility. For this text is situated at the level of the ostentatiously factitious. *Bel-Ami* does not claim to set before the reader's glance a windowpane-like language gesturing toward pure, uncoded reality; rather it intercepts that glance by means of a tain and, mirrorlike, reverses its referential quest upon itself. What it sets before the reader is a nothingness, as I hope to have shown. Illusion has now become substance.

Thus, the mirror, the disguise, and the propensity for make-believe all constitute the codes of the artificial or the insubstantial in *Bel-Ami*. "To appear or not to appear," that is this novel's question. We may conclude that in this limited sense Maupassant has outmastered his master Flaubert, for not only has he truly written "a book about nothing," but he has also mirrored the nothingness of a certain type of writing.

5. Roland Barthes, "L'Effet de réel," *Communications*, XI (1968), 84–89. This article was translated as "The Reality Effect" in Tzvetan Todorov (ed.) *French Literary Theory Today* (Cambridge, England, 1982), 11–17.
6. Philippe Hamon, "Un Discours contraint," in T. Todorov (ed.), *Littérature et réalité* (Paris, 1984), 119–81.

Afterword

The contemplation of illusion and of the flight into its various manifestations links the essays in this collection. They point to a common obsession that transcends schools and the periodizations of literary history. The preoccupation with the ideal as a perfection of reality can be traced back to Rousseau, to be sure; yet, if we look ahead to the *fin-de-siècle* and beyond, we shall find a similar thrust. Beyond the time of Romanticism and Realism, the ultimate nostalgia for the ideal—by means of its systematic refusal of the vulgarities of the real, and its concomitant elevation of the artificial—would find expression in *la décadence*. Indeed, in *Le Vice suprême* of 1896, a novel that Barbey d'Aurevilly's preface summarized as the story of "la race latine qui se meurt" 'the dying Latin race,' Joséphin Péladan depicted his heroine, the Princess Leonora d'Este, in language that both synthesizes and surpasses the Stendhalian and the Flaubertian, the Romantic and the Realistic: "Elle songe. . . . Dans quelle contrée du pays bleu, à la porte de quel paradis perdu, son désir bat-il de l'aile? Sur la croupe de quelle chimère, prend-elle son envolée dans le rêve?" 'She muses. . . . In what land of reverie, at the gate of what paradise lost does her desire's wing flutter? On the back of what chimaera does she take flight into dream?'

Etymologically, decadence signifies a "falling away" from some presumed standard—a deterioration—and if we accent the second syllable of the word in English, we shall hear its component meaning of "decay." But this new, post-Romantic world-weariness, induced by the excesses of the age's obsequies to determinism and scientism, does not merely find expression in *fin-de-siècle* lassitude or in the global rejection of a presumably exsanguine civilization. Indices of Spenglerian decline, or at least what was then understood to constitute it, can be traced throughout Western European literature. The most often-cited examples are the numerous ephemeral "little reviews" of the 1880s—*Le Décadent*, *La Vogue*, *La Revue Wagnérienne*, and so on. But there is also Cavafy's magnificent poem "Waiting for the Barbarians," and *Dorian Gray*, the *Yellow Book*, and even Gilbert and Sullivan's *Patience*. It can be argued that decadence, with its emphasis on the artificial, represents a mineralization of the ideal, and so a reifying process. Thus, Huysmans' *A Rebours* would be the extreme case of a movement that could be clearly detected twenty or more years earlier in the instance of Flaubert's *Salammbô*. If this were entirely true, then futility and pessimism would be the terminus of the quest for the ideal, and hyperestheticism would lead only into artistic culs-de-sac, or to a problematic faith under "skies no longer lighted by the consoling beacons of the ancient hope," as Des Esseintes puts it on the last page of *A Rebours*. The choice seemed to be between sterility on one hand, and obeisance to a rediscovered spirituality on the other. As we know, Huysmans chose the latter path; indeed, his conversion was far from standing as an isolated example at the turn of the century, when even so independent a spirit as Gide was to be tempted (and irritated) by the reassurance and security of the faith of Claudel.

And yet, another, royal way was to open before the insistent quest for the ideal, and here again we may locate its beginnings in Rousseau. For Rousseau emphasized the redeeming, the *creative* dimension of his chimaerical pursuits. As artistic creation in the course of the nineteenth century was to find its focus progressively restricted to this seemingly narrow—yet immediately accessible—aspect of its nature, it would discover *pari passu* a fascination with its own structures and processes. This awareness is best exemplified in painting, where the artist's eye renounced its Realistic window on reality—mimesis—the better to seize on the surface activity of the canvas itself. Such is the history of painting in its rapid evolution from Impressionism to the earliest examples of Expressionism. In literature the result is equally rich—much too rich for all but the slightest adumbration in these closing words. Fiction's incapacity for fulfillment in what it persistently called "reality" simply led it to the novel of the artist, the *Kunstlerroman*, the *roman de l'artiste*, which is to say, to Joyce in English letters, to Thomas Mann in German, to Proust in French. The pursuit of the chimaera ultimately gestures to the artistic quest itself.

Index